Trish Deseine

cooking with friends

For Paddy Brown, Ian and David Stevens. My best friends.

warning

A few recipes include raw eggs. Be sure that the eggs are as fresh as possible. If in any doubt, consult your doctor.

acknowledgments

To all the Marabout team. To Marie-Pierre, for her professionalism. To Hubert and Virginie, and all the hard core of friends and all the guinea pigs that have sat at my table.

To Jacqueline, for her energy and her good humor. To Michel Perron of the *La Galiote* restaurant for his inspiration, and, above all, to Thierry, Coco, Tim, Tanguy, and Victoire for the support they have given me during this project.

Crockery and accessories: Muji, 47, rue des Francs Bourgeois, 75004 Paris, pages 13, 33, 41, 43, 50, 58, 59, 63, 67, 72, 74, 100, 101, 103, 104, 107, 108, 109, 112, 115, 119, 121, 122, 125, 126, 127, 129, 133, 135, 139, 142, 143, 146, 150, 151, 152, 153, 170, 179,

Chône, 60, rue Vieille-du-Temple, 75004 Paris, Tel. 00 33 (0)1 44 78 90 00, pages 72, 81, 104, 122,

Table, 97, rue Vieille-du-Temple, 75004 Paris, pages 63, 136, 147, 149,

Mis en Demeure, 27, rue du Cherche-Midi, 75006 Paris, Tel. 00 33 (0)1 45 48 83 79 pages 51, 63, 101, 105, 107, 133,

Sia France, 78640 Villiers-St-Frédéric, Tel. 00 33 (0)1 34 91 08 00, pages 93, 98, 111,

Une journée en France, place Victorien-Sardou, 78160 Marly-le-Roy, Tel. 00 33 (0)1 30 08 61 31, pages 54, 163.

Fruit and vegetables: Les Jardins de Lætitia, place du Marché, 78200 Mantes-la-Jolie.

This edition published by Silverback Books, Inc., San Francisco.

Editors: Isabelle Jeuge-Maynart and Ghislaine Stora – Artistic editors: Emmanuel Le Vallois and Sophie Coupard.
Proofreaders: Fella Saïdi-Tournoux and Élizabeth Guillon – Production: Gérard Piassale and Laurence Recchia.
North American Version © 2003 Silverback Books, Inc.

Translation supplied by First Edition Translations Ltd, Cambridge, in conjunction with Book Production Consultants plc, Cambridge.

ISBN: 2 501035712
Registration of copyright: no. 17257 / November 2001

Printed in Singapore by Tien Wah Press.

cooking with friends

Trish Deseine

Photography by Marie-Pierre Morel

contents

A book for food-lovers

Like you, Trish is a great food-lover. She appreciates the good things in life and likes to share them. She was a cooking enthusiast from her early childhood days, and it was through watching her mother and grandmother that she came to know from a very young age how to select the best products and to understand the importance of an action or a measurement in pastry-making.

Trish has never stopped improving her expertise by learning from pastry-makers, master chocolate-makers, and chefs. She has managed to adapt their techniques to working in her own kitchen, simplifying them without losing their essence. That way, it's easy for anybody to give Trish's tasty dishes a festive feel.

Feel free to reinvent! Transform your cooking from the everyday, depending on the mood of the moment! Today, thanks to exotic produce, our cuisine is enriched with new flavors. Butchers, fish shops, fruit and vegetable stores, cheese merchants, delicatessens, farmers' markets, as well as supermarkets, make it increasingly easy for us to follow these original recipes.

In this book, Trish gives us some of her recipes "for success" that will get your mouth watering, change your habits for the better, and most of all will enable you to interpret the recipes as you wish, depending on your guests or quite simply the space in your fridge.

In a simple yet stylish way, using no complicated techniques, this book will help you entertain guests, whatever the occasion, all year round.

a picnic
with friends

10 tips to take the stress out of al fresco entertaining!

1
Warn your friends when you invite them that you reserve the right to cancel on the day if the weather is too bad.

2
Devise a fun dish if there are going to be children there. Put up a table for them, but do not force them to remain seated after their first dish. All they will want to do is play, which will leave you free to enjoy your meal in peace.
To regain the balance, serve a joint dessert.

3
If you are going to suggest everybody brings something, tell people well in advance, basing your request on their individual wishes and skills. A cooking enthusiast will be proud to bring their superb *tiramisu*, whereas the culinary novice can always buy the bread and so on.

4
Take care to ask them to bring only dishes that can survive in a cooler or that will not spill in transit.

5
Provide enough salad bowls and dishes for all the contributions. Nine times out of ten, they come in assorted plastic containers.

6
Above all, do not ask people to bring wine: 20 different bottles will ensure that everyone has a massive hangover the next day.

7
Put ice cubes in a large tub or a (disguised!) trashcan to keep drinks cold yet within easy reach.

8
Forget paper or plastic plates and glasses. All your efforts in the kitchen will be for nothing when trying to eat from a floppy, buckling plate. The same goes for the wine! Go to a discount store and buy a set of very plain plates and glasses.

9
If there are more than 20 of you, rent the dishware (it really isn't expensive). Enlist help, otherwise you will spend your whole time running between the kitchen and the garden or the patio and your buffet meal will look like nothing on earth after half an hour.

10
If you are planning to have your picnic in the countryside or on the beach, it is essential to follow point no. 8.

Salads and sandwiches

Baby spinach and bacon salad

Serves 4
Preparation time: 15 minutes
1½ cups frozen peas
4 slices of bacon
9 oz baby spinach leaves, washed
5 oz Monterey Jack cheese, finely sliced
1 tbsp Worcestershire sauce
3 tbsp olive oil
Sea salt and black pepper

Steam or boil the peas in salted water for no longer than 2 or 3 minutes. They should still be firm. Refresh under cold water, then leave to cool completely. Grill the bacon slices until crisp and golden. Combine all the ingredients.
To make the dressing, combine the Worcestershire sauce with the oil, pepper, and sea salt, and serve separately.

Tip. If you have no Monterey Jack, you could use any hard, well-flavored cheese instead. Use any bacon you prefer, but definitely not cured ham. You could use balsamic vinegar as an alternative to the Worcestershire sauce

Beef and bell pepper salad

Serves 6
Preparation time: 15 minutes
Cooking time: 30 minutes for the peppers and 5 minutes for the meat
7 oz sirloin steak
3 bell peppers (red, green, yellow or orange), seeded, broiled, and cut into strips
½ red chile, seeded and finely diced (optional)
1 tsp olive oil
2 tbsp olive oil
A handful of unsalted roasted peanuts
Sea salt and pepper

Fry the meat in 2 tablespoons of the olive oil over high heat. Leave to cool, then slice into thin strips. Combine all the remaining ingredients to make a salad. Serve warm or cold.
If you do include the hot chile in the dressing, warn your guests beforehand to avoid ruining their meal.

Tip. To broil the bell peppers, cut them in half widthwise, place under a very hot broiler, and cook until the skin blisters. Transfer them to a plastic bag and leave them to sweat; this makes them much easier to peel. Alternatively, you can buy a jar of roasted bell peppers.

Beet and chicken liver salad

Serves 6
Preparation time: 10 minutes
Cooking time: 5 minutes
6 chicken livers
3 beets
4 tbsp balsamic vinegar
2 tbsp chopped parsley
3 tbsp olive oil
Salt and pepper

Brown the chicken livers in a very hot skillet with a little olive oil. Set aside. Deglaze the skillet with 2 tablespoons of balsamic vinegar and return the livers to the skillet.
Slice the livers and the beets as finely as possible. Arrange the salad, alternating the chicken liver and beet slices. Make a dressing with the parsley and remaining olive oil and vinegar. Season to taste and serve.
Beet and chicken livers make a delicious combination. Take care not to overcook the livers—they should still be decidedly pink and soft inside.

Tip. Deglazing is a professional term for a very simple and extremely useful process. Remove the meat, then add very hot water or vinegar (very good vinegar, please!) to the burning-hot skillet or roasting pan, and stir vigorously to loosen the congealed cooking sediments and dilute the cooking juices. This way, you will be able to separate and thus remove much of the fat from the skillet, concentrating the aromas to make a delicious sauce or base for a sauce.

Carrot and cilantro salad

Serves 6
Preparation time: 10 minutes
6 carrots
3 tbsp olive oil
1 garlic clove, finely chopped
Juice of 2 limes
2 tbsp chopped cilantro
Sea salt and white pepper

Wash, peel, and finely grate the carrots. Beat the olive oil together with the garlic and lime juice. Add the cilantro. Season just before serving.

Baby spinach and bacon salad

Beef and bell pepper salad

Beet and chicken liver salad

Carrot and cilantro salad

13

Arugula and prosciutto salad

Serves 6
Preparation time: 5 minutes
1 firm melon
6 slices of *prosciutto*
3 good handfuls of arugula
6 tbsp balsamic vinegar dressing (p. 178)

Slice the melon and remove the seeds. Remove the skin and cut the slices into thin strips. Peel off the slices of *prosciutto*. Place alternate layers of arugula, melon, and *prosciutto* in a glass to form spirals. Pour over the dressing when ready to serve.

Suggestion. Add other summer fruits such as apricots or peaches. It looks pretty if you vary the shape of the dishes on the buffet if you are entertaining, and it's fun to take these individual salads with you if you are going off to the countryside or the beach. It's best to use tall glasses.

Mushrooms marinated in olive oil with filberts

Serves 6
Preparation time: 15 minutes
Refrigeration time: 2 hours
11 oz small mushrooms
¾–1 cup olive oil
2 tbsp filberts, coarsely chopped
Sea salt and black pepper

Slice the mushrooms very finely. Combine with the oil, salt, and pepper, and leave to marinate in a refrigerator for 2 hours. Sprinkle with the filberts before serving.

Tip. Try to serve the mushrooms in a very shallow bowl so that they do not look like soup. You can use other flavored oils instead of olive oil. Slightly more "unusual" oils, such as hazelnut oil and almond oil, are becoming ever more readily available in the shops. They would go particularly well with this appetizer.

A salad of flowers

Serves 4
Preparation time: 10 minutes
Picking time: 15 minutes
4 handfuls of lettuce
4 handfuls of edible mixed flowers (roses, nasturtium, begonias, geraniums, daisies, marigolds…)
2 tbsp dressing made with thyme, rosemary, and wine vinegar (p. 178)

Combine the lettuce with the flower petals.
Serve the dressing separately.
Many flowers are edible, some are even delicious; but make sure that you eat only those that you have grown yourself or that are sold for consumption!

Tip. The light green of the lettuce goes well with the colors of the flowers. Try to find or borrow a glass bowl with feet; the flowers look very pretty through the glass!

Potato salad

Serves 4
Preparation time: 10 minutes
Cooking time: 20 minutes
2 red onions
1 tbsp olive oil
A dozen smooth-skinned potatoes
2 small radicchio lettuce hearts
2 tsp pink peppercorns
2 tbsp dressing made with thyme, rosemary, and wine vinegar (p. 178)

Brown the onions in the hot olive oil. Steam the potatoes in their skins, then leave them to cool. Cover a large, shallow dish with the washed and dried lettuce, pile the potatoes in the middle, then the onions, and finally the peppercorns. Serve the dressing separately.

Arugula and *prosciutto* salad

Mushrooms marinated in olive oil

Salad of flowers

Potato salad

Clafouti of broiled
vegetables with red pesto

Prosciutto and fruit slices

Clafouti with broiled vegetables and red pesto

Serves 6
Preparation time: 45 minutes
Cooking time: 30 minutes
14 oz vegetables (bell peppers, zucchini, eggplant, tomatoes, onions)
4 whole eggs
1 egg yolk
1⅔ cups light cream
1¼ cups milk
2 tbsp all-purpose flour
1¼ cups freshly grated Parmesan cheese
3 tbsp red pesto (p. 174)

Cut the vegetables into small pieces, sprinkle with olive oil, and place under the broiler for about 40 minutes. Season with salt and pepper. Drain if necessary and transfer to a shallow ovenproof dish. Preheat the oven to 360° F. Beat the eggs and the yolk with the milk and cream. Add the sifted flour and the Parmesan, and season to taste. Pour over the vegetables and bake for about 30 minutes. Spread the pesto over the top and serve hot, warm, or cold.

Prosciutto and fruit slices with mustard sauce

Serves 4
Preparation time: 10 minutes
Cooking time: 5 minutes
1 loaf of crusty white bread
8 very thin slices of *prosciutto*
1 nectarine
1 fig
1 peach
1 melon
1¼ cups red wine
½ cup sugar
1 tbsp good strong mustard
1 bay leaf
Sea salt and white pepper

Place the wine, sugar, and bay leaf in a pan and boil to produce a light syrup. Add the mustard and beat until incorporated. Cut the fruit into strips and arrange on a slice of bread moistened with olive oil. Peel off the ham and place on the fruits. Pour the sauce around, season to taste, and serve.

Tip. Mustard sauce often comes to my rescue with improvised summer meals. It immediately makes the traditional raw ham/melon just that bit more special. But although this sauce can easily liven up bland fruits, only top quality fruits should be used for this dish!

Real tabbouleh

Serves 6 to 8
Preparation time: 30 minutes
Standing time: 2 hours
½ cup bulgur wheat
8 tomatoes
6 shallots
5 bunches Italian (flat-leaf) parsley
2 bunches fresh mint
Juice of 6 lemons
12 tbsp olive oil

Soak the bulgur wheat for 15 minutes in some warm water with 1 tsp lemon juice. Drain well and dry in a dish towel (yes, that's right, a dish towel). Peel and finely dice the tomatoes, and chop the shallots, parsley, and mint very finely. Combine all these ingredients with the bulgur wheat in the serving dish. Sprinkle with olive oil and lemon juice, season to taste, and leave to stand for at least 2 hours. Before serving, adjust the seasoning and stir gently, adding more lemon juice and/or olive oil if necessary. This dish is simple to prepare and bears no resemblance to its ready-made equivalents. I know chopping all these herbs does take a lot of time, but it really is worth making it yourself.

Tip. Do not try to make this dish with the meager plastic bags of fresh herbs available from supermarkets. If you cannot get beautiful bunches of fresh herbs from your store or farmers' market, make something else instead.

Real tabbouleh

Sweet and savory tarts

Double chocolate raspberry tartlets

Red onion tart

Sweet-and-sour roast vegetable tart

Double chocolate raspberry tartlets

Makes 6
Preparation time: 10 minutes
Cooking time: 20 minutes
9 oz chocolate sweet pastry (p. 182)
7 oz good quality white chocolate
1⅔ cups light cream
9 oz raspberries

Roll out the pastry, and cut out 6 circles to fit tartlet pans roughly 4 in in diameter. Bake blind (see right). Set aside in a cool place. Melt the white chocolate, and add the cream, stirring constantly. Leave to cool slightly—but not too much, as the cream must still be fluid enough to pour into the tartlet shells. Fill the shells with the mixture and place the raspberries evenly on top, allowing them to sink in slightly. Keep in a cool place.

Red onion tart

Serves 6
Preparation time: 10 minutes
Total cooking time: 1 hour 10 minutes
Plain pastry (p. 182)
½ stick butter
1 tbsp olive oil
4 or 5 red onions
3 whole eggs
2 egg yolks
1¼ cups light cream
Salt and pepper

Preheat the oven to 360° F. Roll out the pastry and line a 9-inch baking pan. Bake blind for 15 minutes. Meanwhile, heat the butter and oil in a pan, then add the chopped onions. Cook gently for 20 minutes until they become soft and slightly caramelized. Beat the eggs and the egg yolks together with the cream. Add the onions and pour over the base of the tart. Bake for 30 to 35 minutes.

Sweet-and-sour roast vegetable tart

Serves 6
Preparation time: 1 hour
Cooking time: 20 minutes
9 oz plain pastry (p. 182)
Cold roasted vegetables (p. 176)
1 tbsp lavender or rosemary honey
3 tbsp olive oil
1 tbsp red wine vinegar
A small handful of ground or finely chopped filberts
Sprigs of rosemary and thyme
Sea salt and black pepper

Roll the pastry out and line a greased loaf pan. Bake the pastry blind for 20 minutes and leave to cool. Combine the honey, vinegar, and oil. Gently toss the vegetables in this dressing and add the filberts. Transfer the vegetables to the tart shell, season to taste, garnish with the rosemary and thyme, and serve.

Tip. Baking "blind" means cooking a pastry shell without any filling. To prevent it from puffing up, the base needs to be filled with dried beans or baking beans (p. 160). The advantage of the latter is that they diffuse the heat, thus cooking the pastry base as well as the sides exposed to the heat of the oven. Whether you use dried beans or proper baking beans, you need to make sure you remove them before adding the filling if your guests are to retain their beautiful and expensive crowns!
You can use finely chopped or sliced almonds instead of the filberts. Try using differently shaped baking pans. They may look better and be easier to cut and serve from.

Plum and butter tart

Serves 6
Preparation time: 15 minutes
Cooking time: 25 minutes
11 oz sweet pastry
1½ lbs plums
1 tbsp brown sugar
1 tbsp butter

Preheat the oven to 360° F. Make the sweet pastry (p.182) and use to line the base of a 9- or 10-inch tart pan. Remove the pits from the plums, slice the fruits in half, and arrange in a regular pattern over the base of the pastry shell. Sprinkle with the sugar and chopped butter, and bake for about 25 minutes.
It is vital to make this recipe as soon as these little plums first appear in the shops at the end of the summer. The season is so short. The sweet pastry made with butter gives this big classic an unforgettable flavor.

Tip. Do not remove the pits from the plums until just before you are going to bake the tart, as otherwise they run the risk of turning brown.

Plum and butter tart

The "Big Al"

Serves 6
Preparation time: 1 hour
Cooking time: 25 minutes
For the cake
7 oz good quality dark chocolate
1¾ sticks butter
4 eggs
¾ cup superfine sugar
1 cup all-purpose flour
1 heaped tsp baking powder
For the pecan/fudge cream
4 oz pecans, finely chopped
8 oz good quality dark chocolate
1 cup light cream
2 tbsp butter
For the glaze (optional)
7 oz good quality dark chocolate
Just under 1 stick butter
7 tbsp water

Preheat the oven to 360° F. To make the cake batter, melt the chocolate in a microwave oven. Add the butter and return to the microwave for 30 seconds if necessary. Beat the eggs with the sugar until the mixture becomes pale. Add the sifted flour and baking powder.

Combine the chocolate, eggs, and flour, and pour the mixture into a deep cake pan. Bake for about 25 minutes. Remove the cake from the oven and leave to cool in the pan for about 5 minutes, then turn out onto a wire rack. When completely cold, cut the cake into three layers.

Heat the cream and the chocolate. Add the butter and stir well with a whisk. Leave to cool. Add the pecan nuts and spread one-third of this mixture over the first layer. Repeat the procedure twice and sprinkle with pecans to decorate. Alternatively, repeat the procedure only once, and then glaze the top layer.

To make the glaze, melt all the ingredients in a microwave oven for 1½ minutes (or simply in a bowl over a pan of hot water). Whisk thoroughly until the ingredients are fully incorporated and the glaze is perfectly smooth. Leave to cool and thicken slightly.

Place the cake on a wire rack on top of a sheet of acetate (p. 144) or a sheet of waxed paper, and carefully cover the cake with the glaze. Using a spatula, spread the glaze over the sides. You can collect any excess from the sheet and spread it back on the cake. Leave to cool completely.

Tip. There is a version for the larger family (the "Big Big Al"). Double the quantities (except for the glaze), make two cakes, and split each cake into two, rather than three, to make four layers. If you are looking for a dessert that will meet with the unanimous approval of adults and children alike, then this is it. A rich marriage between the chocolate, cream, butter, and pecans, all covered with a sumptuous chocolate glaze, this is definitely not something for people allergic to fat or who are hooked on low-fat products. Served with fresh strawberries or raspberries, or with the chilled strawberry soup with Pimms (p. 26), the "Big Al" is sheer delight.

The "Big Al"

New season's strawberries

Strawberry shortcakes

Serves 6
Preparation time: 10 minutes
Cooking time: 35 to 40 minutes
11 oz sweet pastry (p. 182)
1 small carton of mascarpone or
6 tbsp pastry cream (see below)
1¼ lbs strawberries

Preheat the oven to 360° F. Roll out the pastry and cut into shapes (hearts, circles, etc.). Bake for about 35 to 40 minutes. Remove from the oven and leave to cool. Using a teaspoon, spread the mascarpone or the pastry cream over the shapes. Place the whole strawberries lightly on the creamy topping and serve.

Chilled strawberry soup with Pimms

Serves 6
Preparation time: 20 minutes
Refrigeration time: 3 to 4 hours
1¾ lbs strawberries
2 cups Pimms
⅔ cup sugar

Clean and halve or quarter the strawberries. Place in a bowl or deep dish. Boil the Pimms with the sugar for 10 minutes. Leave to stand for 1 or 2 minutes (so that the hot syrup does not crack the dish of strawberries).
Pour the syrup over the strawberries. The heat of the syrup will poach them and make them release their juice. Leave in a refrigerator for 2 to 3 hours to cool completely. Stir gently before serving.

Tip. Pimms is the most British of aperitifs. Traditionally, it is served chilled, mixed with lemon-lime soda or ginger ale, and garnished with a sprig of fresh mint, slices of orange or lemon, and sometimes even cucumber. If you do not have any Pimms you can use a good red wine instead. Serve with the light hazelnut gateau (p. 48).

Cream cheese with a strawberry purée

Serves 4
Preparation time: 5 minutes
1 lb strawberries
1 lb top quality cream cheese
2 tbsp superfine sugar
⅔ cup whipping cream

Coarsely crush the strawberries with the sugar, using a fork, to produce a purée with pieces of fruit. Serve with the cream cheese, adding the sugar and whipping cream if you are an incorrigible glutton!

Suggestion. For a bit of variety, you can use 11 oz strawberries and 5 oz raspberries instead of all strawberries.

Strawberry slices

Serves 4
Preparation time: 10 minutes
4 thick slices of fresh crusty white bread
1 small container mascarpone
12 oz strawberries
4 tsp balsamic vinegar
Freshly ground white or black pepper

Spread the *mascarpone* over the slices of bread.
Coarsely chop the strawberries and place a tablespoonful on each slice, then sprinkle with a little vinegar and pepper.

Pastry cream

For 6 shortbreads
Preparation time: 10 minutes
Cooking time: 5 minutes
1 cup whole milk
3 egg yolks
1 level tbsp all-purpose flour, sifted
¼ cup sugar
1 vanilla bean (optional)

Place the milk in a pan with the split vanilla bean (if used) and bring to the boil. Remove the milk from the heat. Beat the eggs with the sugar and flour until the mixture becomes pale and has doubled in volume. Pour the hot milk over the egg mixture, stirring constantly.
Return the mixture to the heat and cook for about 1 minute. Leave to cool, stirring occasionally. Before removing the vanilla bean, scrape the inside thoroughly to extract all the seeds.

Strawberry shortcake

Chilled strawberry soup with Pimms

V   Cream cheese with
strawberry purée

Strawberry slice

finger food

Sandwiches

THE ADVANTAGE OF THESE RECIPES IS THAT THEY NEED NEITHER CUTLERY NOR CHINA AND ARE EASY TO MANAGE, EVEN FOR THE LESS DEXTROUS OR THOSE WHOSE TEETH ARE NOT QUITE WHAT THEY USED TO BE. THEY ARE "EXTENDABLE" TO MAKE FULL PORTIONS; THEY CAN BE SERVED WITH APERITIFS, AT BRUNCH, AND EVEN HAVE THEIR PLACE ON A PARTY BUFFET TABLE.

TODAY WE CAN BUY BREADS FROM ALL OVER THE WORLD: MEDITERRANEAN PITAS, INDIAN NAAN BREAD, SOFT ENGLISH SANDWICH BREAD, BREAD FROM SCANDINAVIA, ITALIAN CIABATTA… THEY OFTEN HAVE THE ADVANTAGE THAT THEY WILL KEEP FOR SEVERAL WEEKS. HERE ARE A FEW DELICIOUS VARIATIONS, ALL SERVED ON THE SAME PLATE SO THAT YOU CAN TRAVEL THE WORLD WITHOUT MOVING FROM YOUR CHAIR.

Swedish bread and smoked salmon

Serves 6
Preparation time: 5 minutes
6 slices of Scandinavian bread (a soft and slightly sweet bread)
6 to 8 slices of smoked salmon
1 small jar capers
1 small container sour cream
Juice of 1 lemon
Black pepper

Arrange the salmon on the bread. Sprinkle with a few drops of lemon juice, followed by a few capers and some pepper. Add a teaspoonful of sour cream and place a second slice of bread on top. Cut into quarters.

Pita, feta, and olives

Serves 6
Preparation time: 3 minutes
1 packet mini pita breads
1 slice feta cheese
12 pitted olives
Olive oil
Black pepper
Wooden toothpicks

Put the pitas in the oven or a toaster for a few minutes before using them. Halve each pita, then chop or crumble the feta onto one half of each. Drizzle over a few drops of olive oil, sprinkle with 1 or 2 diced olives and the pepper, and top with the remaining pita half. Secure with a toothpick.

English cucumber sandwiches

Serves 6
Preparation time: 10 minutes
6 slices of sandwich bread
1 cucumber
Butter
Salt and white pepper

Peel and cut the cucumber into very thin slices. Lightly butter the slices of bread, arrange two thin layers of cucumber on three of the slices, and season with salt and pepper. Top with the remaining three slices, remove the crusts, and cut the sandwiches into symmetrical triangles.

Sweet-and-savory bagels

Serves 4
Preparation time: 10 minutes
4 bagels
1 large container cream cheese
2 or 3 tsp snipped chives
4 tbsp diced pineapple

Combine the pineapple and chives, and then the cheese, and spread this mixture over the bagel halves.

Swedish bread and smoked salmon

Pita, feta, and olives

English cucumber sandwiches

Sweet-and-savory bagel

A dip party makes a change from the usual guacamole.

DIP THE VEGETABLE STICKS (CUCUMBER, CARROT, CELERY), TORTILLA CHIPS (CHOOSE PLAIN ONES SO AS NOT TO DROWN THE FLAVOR OF THE DIP), OR SLIGHTLY WARM PITA BREAD FOR PEOPLE TO TEAR OFF AS AND WHEN THEY WANT.

Avocado, feta, tomato

Serves 4 to 6
Preparation time: 5 minutes
1 large avocado
Juice of 1 lemon
¾ cup sour cream
2 oz feta cheese
1 large tomato, diced
Black pepper
Tabasco

Mix together the avocado, the lemon juice, and the sour cream. Add the crumbled feta cheese and the diced tomato. Season with Tabasco and black pepper. Serve immediately, because avocado discolors quickly despite the addition of lemon juice.

Onion pickle

Serves 6
Preparation time: 10 minutes
Cooking time: 25 minutes
6 onions
3 tbsp olive oil
1 tbsp superfine sugar
2 tsp *ras el-hanout* (Moroccan spice blend)
Salt and pepper

Peel and finely chop the onions. Fry in the butter and oil over low heat until transparent, continue to fry gently until golden, then sprinkle with the sugar. Keep on cooking until the mixture caramelizes slightly (all this should take about 20 minutes). Transfer the mixture to a food processor, add the *ras el-hanout*, and blend until very smooth. Season with salt and pepper.

Hummus

Serves 6 to 8
Preparation time: 15 minutes
1 can chick peas (garbanzo beans)
3 tbsp *tahini* (sesame seed purée)
1 garlic clove
Juice of 2 lemons
Olive oil
Salt and pepper

Drain and rinse the chick peas, then heat for 10 minutes in boiling water. Mix together with the *tahini*, garlic, lemon juice, salt, pepper, and olive oil in a food processor to produce a very smooth purée.

Tip. Omit the *tahini* and garlic to make the following delicious alternatives.

Hummus and peanut butter

Add 2 tablespoons of crunchy peanut butter and combine with a little water so the mixture is not too dry.

Hummus and broiled bell pepper

Add 1 broiled and peeled bell pepper to the food processor.

Avocado, feta, tomato

Onion pickle and pita bread

Hummus

Hummus and peanut butter

Tartines, bruschetta, and crostini QUITE SIMPLY, THESE ARE JUST SLICES OF BREAD, LIGHTLY TOASTED, SOMETIMES RUBBED WITH GARLIC, AND DRIZZLED WITH A LITTLE OLIVE OIL, WHICH YOU CAN VARY AS MUCH AS YOU LIKE. A SLICED CRUSTY LOAF MAKES GOOD *BRUSCHETTA* AND A BAGUETTE IS GOOD FOR *CROSTINI*. THESE TASTY SNACKS CAN BE SERVED AS CANAPÉS, AS AN APPETIZER, OR EVEN AS A MEAL IN THEIR OWN RIGHT! HERE ARE A FEW VARIATIONS.

Roasted bell peppers, olive oil, and basil

Serves 4
Preparation time: 3 minutes (1 hour's cooking time for the peppers)
4 slices of bread
6 to 8 strips different colored bell peppers
2 to 3 tsp olive oil
A few leaves of fresh basil
Sea salt and freshly ground pepper

Arrange one or two slices of roasted bell pepper (p. 62) on the bread, mixing the colors. Drizzle with a few drops of olive oil and season to taste. Garnish with basil leaves.

Foie gras with fresh and dried figs

Serves 4
Preparation time: 10 minutes
4 slices of bread
1 fresh fig
1 dried fig
2 slices medium-cooked foie gras
Sea salt and white pepper

Chop the figs, place one slice of foie gras on the lightly oiled bread (do not use any garlic), sprinkle with sea salt and white pepper, and top with a teaspoonful of the fig mixture.

Almonds and basil

Serves 4 to 6
Preparation time: 10 minutes
6 slices of toast
1 garlic clove
6 tbsp olive oil
⅔ cup blanched almonds
18 black olives, pitted and chopped
1 tbsp chopped capers
4 to 5 tbsp fresh basil
1 tbsp parsley

Crush the almonds and add the capers, olives, parsley, and basil. Add the olive oil and season to taste. Rub the slices of toast with the garlic and spread with the almond mixture.

Sheep's milk cheese with black cherry jam

Serves 4
Preparation time: 3 minutes
4 slices of bread
4 slices of sheep's milk cheese
4 tsp black cherry jelly

Place one slice of cheese on each slice of bread and top with a spoonful of jelly.

Prosciutto with grapes

Serves 4
Preparation time: 3 minutes
4 slices of bread
4 slices of *prosciutto*
6 to 8 grapes, halved

Place the *prosciutto* on the slices of bread and scatter the halved grapes on top.

Prosciutto, dried apricots, and pine nuts

Serves 4
Preparation time: 3 minutes
4 slices of bread
6 to 8 slices *prosciutto*
6 to 8 dried apricots, coarsely chopped
1 or 2 tbsp pine nuts

Arrange the *prosciutto* on the bread, place the apricots on top, and sprinkle with the pine nuts.

Fresh foie gras

Serves 6
Preparation time: 10 minutes
6 slices of bread, toasted
11 oz good quality fresh foie gras
Sea salt and white pepper

Cut the foie gras into reasonably thick slices, about half an inch, and place on the hot toast. Season with the sea salt and white pepper. You can of course fry the foie gras if your guests are not accustomed to eating it raw.

Pecorino, fresh figs, and honey

Serves 4
Preparation time: 3 minutes
4 slices of bread
4–5 oz *pecorino* cheese (or Parmesan)
2 or 3 fresh figs, finely sliced
2 or 3 tsp honey

Arrange the slices of cheese and fig alternately on the bread, then drizzle the honey on top.

Asparagus, melon, and roasted pine nuts

Serves 6
Preparation time: 10 minutes
Cooking time: 10 minutes
6 slices of toast
8 spears of green asparagus
½ melon
1 tbsp pine nuts

Steam the asparagus for 6 to 8 minutes.
Meanwhile, roast the pine nuts in the oven at 360° F, or cook in a skillet for 3 minutes. Slice the melon into thin strips, drain the asparagus tips, and cut them in half lengthwise. Arrange the two ingredients alternately on the slices of toast and scatter the pine nuts over.

Smoked salmon, salmon roe, and sour cream

Serves 4
Preparation time: 3 minutes
4 slices of bread
5 oz smoked salmon
1 small can salmon roe
4 tsp thick sour cream

Arrange the salmon on the slices of bread, spread with the sour cream and top with the salmon roe.

Coleslaw and beet

Serves 6
Preparation time: 3 minutes
6 slices of toast
1 small container of coleslaw
4 small or 1 large beet

Spread the coleslaw on the toast and top with a slice of beet. Do not prepare this too far in advance, as the beet juice will stain the coleslaw.

Mushrooms, grapes, and parsley

Serves 4
Preparation time: 3 minutes
4 slices of bread
6 to 8 small mushrooms, finely sliced
8 to 10 grapes, halved
A few sprigs of Italian (flat-leaf) parsley
Juice of ½ lemon

Combine the mushroom slices with the lemon juice. Arrange the mushrooms and grapes on the bread slices and top with a sprig of parsley.

Tomatoes, hummus, and roasted garlic

Serves 6
Preparation time: 3 minutes
Cooking time: 15 minutes
6 slices of toast
6 tbsp hummus (p. 32)
6 garlic cloves
6 small tomatoes
Sea salt and pepper

Preheat the oven to 360° F and roast the garlic in its skin for about 15 minutes. Leave to cool. Spoon the hummus onto the bread and top with 2 tomato halves and the roasted garlic. Sprinkle with sea salt and pepper.

Peach and prosciutto

Serves 4
Preparation time: 3 minutes
4 slices of bread
4 slices of *prosciutto*
1 peach (or nectarine), skin on, finely sliced

Arrange the *prosciutto* and peach slices alternately on the bread.

Dried pear and Roquefort

Serves 4
Preparation time: 3 minutes
4 slices of bread
4 slices of dried pear
4 oz Roquefort (or any other blue cheese)

Place a slice of pear on the bread and top with a roughly crumbled piece of Roquefort.

Baby spinach leaves, prosciutto, and grapes

Serves 6
Preparation time: 3 minutes
6 slices of toast
6 baby spinach leaves
3 slices of *prosciutto*
6 to 8 grapes

Place one baby spinach leaf on the toast to act as a "small dish" and fill with the ham and grapes.

Breakfast

Scrambled eggs, bacon, and mushrooms

Serves 2
Cooking time: 10 minutes
4 eggs
1 tbsp milk
2 slices of bacon
6 or 7 small mushrooms
Butter
Fresh parsley

Beat the eggs and milk and cook very gently in a nonstick skillet, carefully drawing back the edges as they cook. Season to taste, then remove from the heat just before the end, as the eggs dry out very quickly. Fry the sliced mushrooms in a little butter. In another skillet, fry the bacon. Pat the mushrooms and bacon with kitchen towels to absorb excess fat.

Tip. You can either chop the mushrooms and bacon up small and stir them into the scrambled eggs or place a slice of bacon on the eggs, and top with the mushrooms and a sprinkling of parsley. You will need cutlery to eat the second version, but it does look more attractive.

Scrambled eggs, bacon, and mushrooms

Petits-fours with cheese and dried fruits

I WOULD SUGGEST THESE SAVORY PETITS-FOURS FOR ANY TIME, EITHER WITH AN APERITIF, OR TO REPLACE THE VERY FILLING AND EVER-PRESENT CHEESE BOARD. YOU CAN ALSO SERVE THEM ON SEVERAL SMALL PLATES AS THOUGH THEY WERE THE SWEET PETITS-FOURS OFFERED IN GOOD RESTAURANTS AFTER THE DESSERT.

Dates stuffed with foie gras

Serves 6
Preparation time: 15 minutes
1 package of pitted dates
5 oz medium-cooked foie gras
Sea salt and white pepper

Place pieces of foie gras in the dates.
Sprinkle a few grains of sea salt and a little pepper over the foie gras just before serving.

Apricots and prunes with blue cheese (Roquefort, Gorgonzola, Stilton)

Depending on the strength of the cheese, combine it with a little sour cream or mascarpone. Make an opening at the top of the prunes and along the side of the apricots and fill with the cheese mixture.

Parmesan with pine nuts

Grate some fresh Parmesan cheese and combine it with some cream cheese. Shape into small balls and roll them in the pine nuts.

Goat's cheese with chopped filberts or almonds

Shape the goat's cheese into little balls, then roll them in the chopped and toasted filberts.

Goat's cheese with raisins

Repeat the above procedure using raisins.

Parmesan cheese with pecans or walnuts

Grate the fresh Parmesan cheese and combine it with some cream cheese.
Shape into small mounds and place 3 pecan halves around the sides and on top.

Dates stuffed with foie gras

Apricots and prunes with blue cheese

Parmesan with pine nuts

Goat's cheese with chopped filberts or almonds.
Parmesan cheese with pecans or walnuts. Goat's cheese with raisins

Four fillings for stuffed cherry tomatoes

Spice-fried nuts

Four fillings for stuffed cherry tomatoes

They are irresistible. It really is wonderful to be able to eat both the contents and the container at the same time.

What's more, nowadays they come in a variety of different sizes, often very fragrant. It's true that it takes a bit of time to remove the seeds, but there is a tool specially designed for that purpose (p. 160). Leave the stem on the lid and place it on top of or alongside the stuffed tomato. It looks pretty and that is the part that is so fragrant!

Serves 6 to 8
Preparation time: 35 minutes
32 small tomatoes (8 for each filling)

Salmon

1 small container of salmon pâté
1 small container of salmon roe

Stuff the tomato with the salmon and top with a sprinkling of salmon roe.

Tapenade

1 small container of tapenade (olive and anchovy paste)
Basil leaves

Spoon the tapenade into the tomatoes and garnish with some fresh basil.

Ricotta and chives

¼ cup ricotta (or cottage cheese)
1 tsp finely chopped chives
Salt and pepper

Combine the ingredients and spoon into the tomatoes.

Scrambled eggs and ham

2 eggs, scrambled (see p. 38)
1 slice prosciutto

Cut the ham into small pieces, combine with the eggs, and spoon into the tomatoes.

Spice-fried nuts

Serves 6
Preparation time: 3 minutes
Cooking time: 5 minutes
9 oz unsalted blanched nuts (almonds, filberts, pecans, cashews, macadamia nuts, peanuts)
1 tsp mixed spices (cumin, cinnamon, nutmeg, curry, etc.)
Sea salt

Toast the nuts in a skillet with the spices for a few minutes. Add the sea salt and stir before serving.

Puff pastry twists

Sesame and poppy seed

Serves 6
Preparation time: 10 minutes
Cooking time: 10 minutes
1 block of puff pastry
2 tbsp sesame seeds
2 tbsp poppy seeds
1 egg

Preheat the oven to 400° F. Roll out a block of puff pastry and brush with the beaten egg. Scatter the poppy and sesame seeds over the pastry, pressing them into the pastry. Cut the pastry into ⅝-inch wide strips, then twist. Brush again with a little egg. Bake on a greased baking sheet for 8 to 10 minutes.

Anchovy

Serves 6
Preparation time: 10 minutes
Cooking time: 10 minutes
1 block of puff pastry
1 small can anchovies in olive oil
2 tbsp olive oil
1 egg

Roll out the puff pastry, cut in two lengthwise, and brush with beaten egg. Mash the anchovies in a little olive oil, spread this mixture over one of the pastry halves, and cover with the remaining piece of pastry. Then proceed as for the previous recipe.

Cheese

Serves 6
Preparation time: 10 minutes
Cooking time: 10 minutes
1 block of puff pastry
5 to 6 tbsp grated cheese
(*pecorino*, Cheddar, *manchego*, *gruyère*)
1 egg, beaten

This recipe substitutes one of the cheeses for the anchovies. Press the edges of the pastry down firmly so that the cheese does not run out.

Puff pastry twists: sesame and poppy
seeds, anchovy, cheese

Traditional fruit cakes and sponges

Dried fruit tea loaf

Lemon cake

Light hazelnut gateau

Dried fruit tea loaf

Serves 6 to 8
Preparation time: 30 minutes
Cooking time: 1½ hours
Soaking time for the dried fruits: 1 night
1 lb all-purpose flour, sifted
2 cups golden raisins
2 cups currants
13 fl oz hot tea
1 cup brown sugar
3 rounded tsp baking powder
1 egg
1 tsp mixed spice

The evening before you are going to bake the loaf, pour the hot tea over the dried fruit and leave to soak overnight. The next day, preheat the oven to 340° F. Mix together the beaten egg, mixed spice, baking powder, sugar, flour, tea, and dried fruit. Transfer this mixture to a greased 7-inch loaf pan. Bake for 1½ hours. Remove from the oven and leave to cool in the pan for 5 minutes before turning out onto a wire rack.

Tip. Serve hot or cold with butter.

Lemon cake

Serves 6 to 8
Preparation time: 15 minutes
Cooking time: 45 minutes
½ stick butter, softened
½ cup + 2 tbsp sugar
1⅛ cups all-purpose flour
3 rounded tsp baking powder
½ cup milk
2 eggs
Juice and zest of 1 lemon
2½ tsp sugar

Preheat the oven to 340° F. Beat the butter and sugar until pale and fluffy. Combine the eggs and milk, and gradually add this mixture alternately with the flour and baking powder to the butter and sugar mixture. Add the lemon zest. Transfer to a greased 9-inch loaf pan and bake for 45 minutes. Remove from the oven and pour the sweetened lemon juice over the top of the cake. Leave to cool in the pan.

Tip. If you really want to go overboard with the lemon, serve with lemon curd (p.52).

Light hazelnut gateau

Serves 6 to 8
Preparation time: 15 minutes
Cooking time: 30 minutes
5 egg whites
1 stick butter, melted
1 cup ground hazelnuts (filberts)
½ cup + 2 tbsp sugar
⅔ cup all-purpose flour

Preheat the oven to 400° F. Whisk the egg whites into stiff peaks. Gently fold in the hazelnuts and sugar. Then add the flour and lastly the melted butter. Transfer the mixture to a greased cake pan and bake for 15 minutes. Lower the temperature to 300° F, and cook for a further 15 minutes approximately.

Tip. For the almond version, use 1 cup ground almonds instead of the hazelnuts and omit one egg white.

Butter shortbread

Serves 6 to 8
Preparation time: 15 minutes
Cooking time: 50 minutes
2¼ sticks cold butter, cut into small pieces
¾ cup sugar
2⅔ cups all-purpose flour

Preheat the oven to 300° F. Work all the ingredients together using your fingertips or a food processor until the mixture resembles breadcrumbs. Knead for 1 minute on a cold, lightly floured surface. Press the mixture out in a fluted tart pan and bake for 50 minutes. Remove from the oven, cut into triangles, and sprinkle with sugar. Leave to cool in the pan.

Walnut shortbread

Serves 6 to 8
Preparation time: 15 minutes
Cooking time: 30 minutes
1 cup walnuts
1 stick butter
7½ tbsp superfine sugar
1½ cups all-purpose flour

Preheat the oven to 300° F. Beat the butter and sugar until pale and fluffy. Add the flour and nuts. Transfer the mixture to a tart pan and press the mixture down gently with your fingers. Bake for 30 minutes. Remove from the oven and leave to cool in the pan.

Butter shortbread

Jam in a jiffy

Caramel spread

Double strawberry jam

Lemon curd

Caramel spread

Cooking time: 3 hours
1 can sweetened condensed milk

Make a very small hole in the top of the can. Place the can in a pan of water. Bring to the boil and simmer for 3 hours. The milk will caramelize. Leave to cool and serve.

Double strawberry jam

Makes about 10 jars
Preparation time: 30 minutes
Cooking time: 6 minutes
5½ lbs strawberries
Juice of ½ lemon
5½ lbs sugar

Quickly rinse the fruits. Shake dry. Hull and chop the strawberries. Place in a large pan and add the sugar and lemon juice. Leave to soak, stirring occasionally. Quickly bring to the boil over high heat and cook for 6 minutes, stirring constantly with a long-handled wooden spoon. Test for a set by dropping a little on a cold saucer to see if it wrinkles when pushed with your finger. Pour into clean, dry jars. Fill almost to the top, screw on the lids, and turn the jars over as they cool. Instead, you can put a circle of waxed paper on the jam, then a cellophane jelly cover held on by an elastic band.

Lemon curd

Makes 2 small jars
Preparation time: 15 minutes
Cooking time: 20 minutes
⅔ cup sugar
Zest and juice of two large lemons
4 eggs
A knob of butter

Carefully grate the lemon zest, then extract the juice from the lemons using a lemon squeezer. In a bowl, combine the juice and the eggs, then add the sugar. Cut the butter into small pieces and add to the mixture, then cook in a bowl placed over a pan of hot water. Stir frequently for 20 minutes until the mixture thickens. Leave to cool, stirring occasionally.

Suggestion. Lemon curd makes a perfect filling for a lemon tart. Blind bake a plain or sweet pastry shell (p. 182). Leave to cool and spread the lemon curd over the base

Apricot and vanilla jam

Makes about 10 jars
Preparation time: 30 minutes
Cooking time: 5 minutes
Soaking time: 10 to 12 hours
6½ lbs apricots
Juice of ½ lemon
5½ lb sugar
3 vanilla beans

Quickly wash the apricots. Remove the pits and cut the fruits into large chunks. Split the vanilla beans in two and then cut each half in two, making 12 pieces. Place the apricots in a large pan and add the sugar, lemon juice, and vanilla pieces. Leave to soak until the sugar has dissolved completely. Cook over high heat for 5 minutes, stirring constantly. Pour into jars, adding a piece of vanilla to each one.

Tip. Choose vanilla beans that are plump, shiny, and supple. Avoid those sold in bags. You can find excellent ones in delicatessens. Vanilla keeps very well in dry conditions. Everyone tells you to keep it in sugar, but rather than having flavored sugar, I prefer to keep it in an air-tight jar in a cool cupboard so that it stays soft.

Apricot and vanilla jam

dining
in the kitchen

1 2 3 4 5
6 7 8 tips to take the stress out of entertaining!

FOR SEVERAL YEARS NOW, IT HAS BEEN THE EPITOME OF STYLE TO INVITE FRIENDS TO EAT IN YOUR KITCHEN. IT'S TRUE THAT THE MOOD THERE IS MORE RELAXED AND WE HAVE NO QUALMS ABOUT TEARING OFF SOME PAPER TOWELS TO USE AS A NAPKIN OR USING THE SAME PLATES AND CUTLERY THROUGHOUT THE MEAL. BUT MEALS SUCH AS THIS OFTEN ENTAIL MORE RESTRICTIONS THAN ADVANTAGES. HERE ARE SOME TIPS…

1
Avoid making dishes that will smoke or stink out your guests. It's not at all pleasant for them to return home and be the only ones smelling of salmon, or cold because the kitchen door had to be left open for most of the evening to air it.

2
There is no room for error. You can no longer rinse the steak under the tap because it has dropped on the floor, nor can you shred the raw ham with your teeth, or eat the scrapings from the bottom of the pan… Your guests are watching you!

3
Serve a filling appetizer, then just one main dish, and possibly a salad.

4
Make soups. I often use them and I invent them all the time. They are tasty because you can concentrate a maximum number of flavors in a minimum amount of liquid. (For a sumptuous mouthful, why not make one with shrimp, for example 1 lb shrimp for 3 helpings), or alternatively a soup that is a meal in itself, full of all sorts of ingredients? Deliciously filling when served with bread and butter.

5
Use the kitchen for any meal that involves equipment (a table-top grill, fondue, pancakes, etc.). This solves the problem of the electric extension cord. You can always escape the smells in the living room!

6
Dining in the kitchen means you can make dishes that you serve at the last minute or that you have to keep a close eye on (pasta, risotto) without missing out on any of the conversation.

7
Why not go the whole hog and set the table with all the trimmings? Even if the location doesn't entirely lend itself to it, use your best silver, have candles, and get out your best napkins.

8
Finally, you really must tidy up the kitchen. There is no question of this room resembling a bombsite, with dirty pans, empty packaging, or the leftovers from the children's meal.

Soups

Fish chowder

Cream of asparagus soup with foie gras

Cream of Stilton and bacon soup

Fish chowder

The word "chowder" comes from the French word *chaudière*, the pan fishermen use to make fish soups.

Serves 6
Preparation time: 20 minutes
Cooking time: 15 minutes
2¼ lb mussels, cleaned
12 clams, in their shells, cleaned
9 oz cod or halibut, cut into pieces
½ stick butter
3 shallots
3½ tbsp all-purpose flour
4 cups fish stock (p. 180)
5 tbsp sour cream
⅔ cup white wine
Salt and pepper
Parsley

Sweat the shallots in the butter until they become transparent. Add the flour and stir for 2 minutes. Add the wine and the fish stock and boil for 2 to 3 minutes. Add the shellfish and cod or halibut and simmer for about 10 minutes. Discard any shellfish that have not opened. Thicken with the sour cream, season to taste, and garnish with the parsley. Serve immediately.

Cream of asparagus soup with foie gras

Serves 6
Preparation time: 15 minutes
Cooking time: 20 minutes
3 bundles of green asparagus
4 cups water
4 cups chicken stock (p. 180)
1 cup light cream
6 slices crusty white bread, toasted
4 oz fresh foie gras
Sea salt and white pepper
Chervil

Discard the woody ends of the asparagus, wash, then cut off the tips. Bring the water and stock to a boil, plunge the stems into the liquid, and cook for 15 to 20 minutes. Halve the tips lengthwise and steam for 4 to 5 minutes. Take care not to overcook them—they should still be firm. Refresh under cold water and set aside. In a food processor or blender, blend the cooked asparagus stems with the cooking liquid, season to taste, then add the cream. Top each slice of toast with the foie gras sprinkled with sea salt and pepper, and scatter with the asparagus tips and a little chervil. Place in the bottom of the bowl and pour the very hot cream soup over it.

Tip. I always use green asparagus. It is easier to cook, has a better flavor, and best of all does not need peeling (unless it has grown beyond a certain height), unlike its paler cousin.

Cream of Stilton and bacon soup

Serves 6
Preparation time: 30 minutes
Cooking time: 20 minutes
14 oz blue Stilton
2 cups light cream
1½ cups milk
2 starchy potatoes
8 slices of bacon
Salt and pepper

Boil or steam the potatoes. Drain, then transfer to a pan with the milk and blend. Broil the bacon lightly. Crumble the Stilton over the potatoes and gently stir it in. When the cheese has melted, add the cream and the salt and pepper. Bring to a boil, then remove from the heat. Cut the bacon into small pieces and place in the bottom of the bowls or in the soup tureen. Serve immediately.

Tip. Before serving, add a dash of sherry or port. You can use any other blue cheese instead of the Stilton.

Cream of cèpe mushrooms and truffle soup

Serves 6
Preparation time: 10 minutes
Cooking time: 20 minutes
1 lb fresh cèpe mushrooms, wiped and coarsely chopped
1 small shallot, finely chopped
1 small can truffles (optional)
4 cups chicken stock (p. 180)
1 tbsp olive oil
1 small container sour cream
1 cup water
1 small container walnut butter (p. 172)
Salt and pepper

Melt the butter in a pan with the olive oil. Add the shallot and the mushrooms. Cook over low heat until the mushrooms have released all their moisture. Add the stock and water, bring to a boil, and cook over low heat for about 15 minutes. Add the truffles, cook for a little longer, then blend in a blender or food processor until very smooth. Add the sour cream, season to taste, stir again, and serve with slices of bread and walnut butter.

Tip. If you are new to truffles, make this soup using a whole truffle (weighing about 1 ounce), but reserve at least half to grate finely over the soup just before serving.

Cream of cepe mushrooms and truffle soup

Soup in four colors

Spinach soup

Serves 6
Preparation time: 5 minutes
Cooking time: 25 minutes
7 oz fresh spinach
2 large starchy potatoes
4 cups vegetable stock (p. 180)
1 cup light cream
¼ stick butter
Salt and pepper

Cut the potatoes into pieces and gently cook with the spinach and butter in a large pan for 2 to 3 minutes. Add the stock and cook over low heat for about 20 minutes.
Blend in a blender, season to taste, add the cream, and serve.

Suggestion. For added flavor, why not grate a pear or Granny Smith apple over the soup just before serving?

Chilled beet and apple soup

Serves 6
Preparation time: 15 minutes
Refrigeration time: 1½ to 2 hours
1½ lbs cooked beets
11 oz Granny Smith apples
2 oz shallots
1 garlic clove (optional)
⅔ cup olive oil
1 tbsp lemon juice
2 cups light cream
Salt and pepper
Cucumber
Chervil

Peel and dice the beets and apples. In a blender or food processor, blend the shallots and garlic to produce a very smooth purée. Add the olive oil, cream, lemon juice, salt, and pepper, and blend. Leave to chill in a refrigerator. Garnish with chervil and diced cucumber.

Yellow soup

Serves 6
Preparation time: 15 minutes
Cooking time: 20 minutes
4 oz pumpkin
1 carrot
2 cups cauliflower florets
½ cup corn kernels (preferably fresh)
1 yellow bell pepper
1 onion
4 cups vegetable stock (p. 180)
¼ stick butter
1 tsp turmeric
Salt and pepper

Chop all the vegetables into small pieces. Melt the butter in a large pan and sweat the vegetables for 2 or 3 minutes. Add the turmeric and the stock. Bring to a boil and simmer for 15 minutes (the vegetables should still be firm). Season to taste and serve.

Chilled roast bell pepper soup

Serves 6
Preparation time: 30 minutes
Cooking time: 1 hour
Refrigeration time: 1½ to 2 hours
6 red bell peppers
6 to 8 ripe tomatoes, skinned and seeded
2 tbsp olive oil
3 shallots, finely chopped
1 garlic clove
4 cups vegetable stock (p. 180)
Tabasco or Worcestershire sauce
Salt and pepper

Preheat the oven to 360° F. Cut the bell peppers in half, remove the seeds, brush with olive oil, and roast, skin side up, for about 1 hour. Remove from the oven and place immediately in a plastic bag to make them easier to peel.
Heat the oil in a large pan and sweat the shallots and garlic. Add the peppers and tomatoes together with the stock. Simmer over low heat for 3 to 4 minutes. Allow the soup to cool, then pass through a blender. Place in a refrigerator. Add the Tabasco or Worcestershire sauce, salt, and pepper. Basil leaves make a good garnish.

Spinach soup

Yellow soup

Chilled roast bell pepper soup

Al dente fresh pasta

Lemon and *pecorino* fettucine

Salmon roe spaghetti

Seafood with squid ink tagliatelle

Lemon and pecorino fettucine

Serves 6
Preparation time: 10 minutes
Cooking time: 10 minutes
1 lb fettucine
2 tbsp lemon zest
¼ stick butter
¼ cup sour cream
2 tbsp grated *pecorino* cheese
1 tbsp pine nuts
Salt and pepper

Boil the fettucine in salted water until *al dente*.
Melt the butter in a pan, then add the lemon zest and the cream.
Bring to a boil, then add the cheese and stir. Pour over the pasta
and sprinkle with the pine nuts.

Salmon roe spaghetti

Serves 6
Preparation time: 5 minutes
Cooking time: 10 minutes
1 lb spaghetti
3 jars salmon roe
1 tbsp dill
½ stick butter
Sea salt and black pepper

Boil the pasta in salted water, drain. Add the butter, salt, and
pepper, and stir. Serve with small dollops of salmon roe and dill
spooned onto the spaghetti.

Seafood with squid ink tagliatelle

Serves 6
Preparation time: 10 minutes
Cooking time: 20 minutes
1 lb squid ink tagliatelle or any other pasta
11 oz seafood (mussels, scallops, squid, etc.)
1 cup dry vermouth
2 shallots
1 tbsp butter
Salt and pepper

Prepare the seafood while the water is coming to a boil for the
pasta. Melt the butter in a large skillet, then sweat the shallots.
Add the seafood, stir well, and pour in the vermouth. Cook for 2
to 3 minutes, season, then keep warm.
Cook the pasta. As soon as it is ready, pour the seafood mixture
over the pasta, stir, and serve immediately.

Tip. Supermarkets sell useful bags of frozen seafood cocktail. You
can cook these from frozen, adding 2 or 3 minutes to the cooking
time. If you are using fresh seafood, it is best to stick to just one
type to make life easier.

Mushroom ravioli

Serves 6
Preparation time: 1 hour
Cooking time: 15 minutes
1 lb very thin sheets of pasta (p. 184)
1 lb mushrooms, chanterelles if possible
½ cup finely chopped shallots
¼ stick butter
1 tbsp olive oil
2 cups light cream
1 tbsp basil
1 tbsp dill
1 tbsp chives
1 tbsp chervil
1 tbsp Italian (flat-leaf) parsley
Salt and pepper

The general rule is that you gently brush the chanterelle
mushrooms, then remove the stems if they are earthy. Personally,
I prefer to rinse them very briefly under running water as well (to
remove any remaining stubborn little grains of soil!). Coarsely
chop the mushrooms. In a skillet, sweat the shallots in the butter
and oil, then add the mushrooms. Leave to cook until the
moisture released by the mushrooms has evaporated. Remove
from the heat, add the chives, and chop very finely. Spoon this
mixture evenly in little mounds over a layer of pasta, slightly
moistening the pasta around each mound. Cover with a second
sheet of pasta, and press down with wet fingers between each
ravioli.
Cut into individual ravioli pieces using a fluted pastry wheel or
ravioli cutter (p. 160).
If you are not going to cook them straight away, cover them well
to prevent them from drying out. Do not put them in the
refrigerator, where they would absorb too much moisture.
Boil for 4 to 5 minutes in salted water.
Coarsely chop the remaining herbs, heat the cream, then add the
herbs, and season. Stir in the ravioli, and sprinkle with freshly
grated Parmesan or pecorino cheese.
Serve immediately.

Suggestion. The addition of cooked and chopped shrimp makes
this filling extra flavorful. Another tasty alternative would be
escargots in a cream sauce with a hint of garlic.

Mushroom ravioli

All about chicken

Tequila chicken

Thai chicken

Chicken broth like mother used to make

Tequila chicken

Serves 6
Preparation time: 15 minutes
Cooking time: 30 minutes
Marinating time: 2 hours
6 free-range chicken pieces
Juice of 5 limes
4 tbsp tequila
6 tortillas
3 tomatoes, skinned and diced
3 avocados
6 lettuce leaves
2 cloves garlic
1 red chile (optional)
5 tbsp olive oil
Salt and pepper

Mix together the lime juice, tequila, 1 finely chopped garlic clove, half the olive oil, the salt and pepper, add the chicken pieces and leave in the refrigerator to marinate for 1 to 2 hours. Finely chop the remaining garlic clove. Put the peeled and diced tomatoes, seeded and chopped chile pepper, if using, the garlic, and a little oil in a large bowl and set aside. Roast or barbecue the chicken. Reheat the tortillas in a conventional or a microwave oven, then fill with the tomatoes, thinly sliced avocados, and lettuce leaves, and serve with the chicken.

Thai chicken

Serves 6
Preparation time: 30 minutes
Cooking time: 1 hour
Marinating time: 1 to 2 hours
1 free-range chicken, about 4 lb in weight
Juice of 1 lime
2 garlic cloves
2 tbsp olive oil
1 tsp sesame oil
1 small can coconut milk
1 tbsp fresh ginger
1 sprig lemongrass
2 tsp Thai seven-spice seasoning
3 tbsp chopped cilantro
2 tbsp fresh chopped basil
Salt and pepper

Combine all the ingredients except the coconut milk, cilantro, and basil, and rub over the chicken. Leave to marinate in a cool place for 1 or 2 hours. Preheat the oven to 475° F. Put the chicken in the oven, and immediately reduce the temperature to 400° F. Cook for about 1 hour, basting frequently. As soon as the chicken is cooked, remove it from the oven and carve, reserving the cooking juices. Keep the chicken warm. Strain the cooking juices to remove the pieces of garlic and ginger, and discard excess fat. Add the coconut milk, season to taste, and gently reheat. When ready to serve, sprinkle with the chopped herbs. Serve with a good Thai rice.

Tip. You can make your own spice blend using red chile pepper, ginger, coriander seeds, cinnamon, cumin, star anise, and cloves. Fresh lemongrass is not always available but you can buy lemongrass paste in delicatessens and supermarkets. It won't matter too much if you have to miss it out altogether!

Chicken broth like mother used to make

New Yorkers call this dish "Jewish penicillin."
In many countries, people have always believed (and still do) that a fortifying, vitamin-packed chicken broth is a better remedy for flu than any other medicine!

Serves 6
Preparation time: 20 minutes
Cooking time: 1½ hours
1 free-range chicken, about 4 lb in weight
1 leek
2 carrots
1 onion
2 stems of celery
3 tbsp chopped parsley
3 tbsp pearl barley
1 tbsp chick peas (garbanzo beans)
1 tbsp split peas
Salt and pepper

Place the whole chicken in a pan and add sufficient water to cover. Bring to a boil, then add the beans, and barley, and onion. Simmer for 1 hour, then add all the vegetables, finely chopped, and the parsley. Season with salt and pepper, and simmer for a further 30 minutes.

Traditional roast chicken

Serves 6
Preparation time: 45 minutes
Cooking time: 1¼ hours
1 free-range chicken, about 4 lb in weight
5 to 7 oz stale white bread
1 large onion
4 tbsp parsley
1¼ sticks butter
4 or 5 slices of bacon

Preheat the oven to 475° F. Place all the ingredients apart from the chicken and bacon in a food processor and chop very finely. Stuff the chicken with this mixture, place the bacon on top of the chicken, then put in the oven, immediately reducing the temperature to 400° F. Cook for about 1¼ hours. Cover the chicken with aluminum foil if the bacon begins to burn. It should remain crisp. Serve with mashed potatoes (p. 170), Brussels sprouts, bread sauce (p. 164), and the stuffing.

Traditional roast chicken

Monkfish korma

Serves 6
Preparation time: 15 minutes
Cooking time: 30 minutes
6 monkfish medallions, weighing about 6 oz each
2 onions
1 tsp saffron threads
⅔ cup boiling water
4 garlic cloves
1 ¾ oz fresh ginger
1 tsp cumin
1 tsp cardamom seeds
1 tsp cinnamon
5 cloves
2 tsp coriander seeds
1 cup cashew nuts (preferably unsalted)
⅓ cup blanched almonds
5 oz plain yogurt
¾ cup sour cream
2 tsp chopped cilantro
1 tbsp olive oil
1 tbsp butter
Salt and pepper

Put the saffron in the boiling water and leave to infuse, off the heat, for 10 minutes. In a food processor, blend the ginger, cashew nuts, cardamom seeds, cloves, coriander seeds, cumin, cinnamon, and yogurt to form a smooth paste. Heat the oil and half the butter in a skillet and fry the fish until golden. In another skillet, fry the onions and garlic in the remaining butter for about 3 minutes until transparent.

Add the spice and yogurt mixture, cook for a few minutes, then add the saffron water. Stir well, then add the fish.

Cook for about 20 minutes. The monkfish should be soft. Lower the heat, add the sour cream and almonds, and slowly return to simmering point. It must not boil, as otherwise the sour cream will separate. Sprinkle with chopped cilantro and serve with naan breads and plain or turmeric-spiced basmati rice.

Turmeric-spiced rice

Serves 6
Preparation time: 5 minutes
Cooking time: 25 minutes
2¼ cups basmati rice
3 tbsp oil
3 cloves
1 bay leaf
2 garlic cloves
½ tsp turmeric
2 tbsp chives
1 tsp salt
Pepper

Rinse the rice two or three times under cold running water and drain well. Heat the oil in a pan, add the cloves, bay leaf, and garlic. As soon as the garlic starts to brown, add the rice and the turmeric, and stir gently for 1 minute. Add 2⅔ cups water, together with the salt, and bring to a boil.

Cover, lower the heat, and simmer gently for 25 minutes. Add the salt and pepper and sprinkle with the finely chopped chives just before serving.

Monkfish korma

Hooked on meat

Loin of lamb with flavored sea salt

Pork chops with apple chutney and apple potato bread

Slow-roast lamb with mint sauce

Loin of lamb with flavored sea salt

Serves 4
Preparation time: 10 minutes
Cooking time: 20 minutes
1 loin of lamb or 8 loin chops
3 tbsp olive oil
2 tbsp sea salt
1 tsp dried lavender seeds (or rosemary, or savory)
1 tsp black pepper

Preheat the oven to 430° F. Combine the salt, pepper, and lavender. Brush the lamb with olive oil, then rub the lavender mixture into the skin.
Roast for 15 to 20 minutes. The meat will be brown on the outside, but pink inside. Cut into individual chops or in fours and arrange alternately to reveal the crossed bones.
Serve with crunchy fresh peas.

Pork chops with apple chutney and apple potato bread

Serves 4
Preparation time: 30 minutes
Cooking time: 15 minutes
4 pork chops
1 lb potatoes
4 tbsp apple chutney (p. 168)
2 baking apples, finely grated
1 cup all-purpose flour
¼ stick butter
Grapeseed oil
Sea salt and pepper

Boil the potatoes in salted water, drain well, then mash, adding some of the butter. Gradually stir in the flour to produce a dough. Dredge a marble slab or a work surface with flour, then roll out the dough until ¼-in thick. Using a glass or a pastry cutter, cut out circles roughly 4 inches in diameter. Spoon the grated apple over half of each circle, fold over, and press the edges together to seal.
Fry these apple turnovers in the butter for 8 minutes. In another skillet, heat the grapeseed oil together with the remaining butter and fry the pork chops. Season with salt and pepper and serve with the chutney.

Slow-roast lamb with mint sauce

Serves 4 to 6
Preparation time: approx. 15 minutes
Cooking time: 2 to 3 hours
Marinating time: 1 to 2 hours
1 lamb shoulder
4 or 5 tbsp olive oil
5 garlic cloves
Sea salt
For the sauce
3 tbsp chopped mint
3 tbsp white wine vinegar
1 tsp sugar
Preheat the oven to 475° F.
Rub the lamb with the garlic and brush with olive oil and salt. Leave to rest in a cool place. Place the meat in a roasting pan in the oven. After 10 minutes, reduce the oven temperature to 300° F. Turn the meat over regularly and baste with the cooking juices as often as possible (about every 30 minutes). The meat is cooked when you can cut it with a spoon.
Mix together the mint, vinegar, and sugar to make traditional English mint sauce, a delicious accompaniment to this melt-in-the-mouth roast lamb.

Tip. Serve with crispy roasted vegetables or mashed potato (p. 170) with olive oil. Follow the same procedure to cook knuckles of lamb. Allow one knuckle for two people and carve at the table. If you don't see them at your butcher's counter, ask him to prepare them for you.

Beef braised in Guinness

Serves 4
Preparation time: 15 minutes
Cooking time: 1½ to 2 hours
1 lb 10 oz braising steak, fat removed, cut into cubes
¼ cup coarsely diced bacon
2 carrots
2 onions, chopped
2 tbsp all-purpose flour
2 cups beef stock
1¼ cups Guinness (or any other Irish stout)
1 tbsp butter
1 tbsp olive oil
1 bouquet garni
Salt and black pepper

Melt the butter and oil in a cast-iron casserole or heavy-bottomed pan and brown the diced bacon, onions, and meat for a few minutes. Sprinkle with the flour and cook for 1 minute. Leave to cool slightly before adding the stock and the stout.
Combine thoroughly and bring to a boil, stirring constantly. Add the bouquet garni and the sliced carrots. Cover and leave to simmer over low heat for 1½ to 2 hours. The meat should be tender. When ready to serve, remove the bouquet garni, adjust the seasoning, and serve with steamed potatoes.

Beef braised in Guinness

... to finish

Double apricot and Stilton lattice pie

Apple and orange crumble

Baked apples with almonds, mascarpone, and honey

Double apricot and Stilton lattice pie

Serves 6
Preparation time: 20 minutes
Cooking time: 20 minutes
10 oz puff pastry
7 oz blue Stilton (or Gorgonzola, Roquefort, etc.)
2 or 3 tbsp light cream
6 to 8 dried apricots, diced
8 fresh apricots, diced
1 egg, beaten
Salt and pepper

Preheat the oven to 360° F. Cut the pastry into two rectangles, one slightly smaller than the other. Roll out the larger one and place on a greased baking sheet.
Crumble the cheese and combine with the cream and the diced apricots. Spread over the pastry and season with salt and pepper.
Roll out the remaining pastry and make the lattice effect on top using a shaped rolling pin (p. 160). Alternatively, make small, regular incisions to create the same effect.
Tease the rectangle out and place on top of the cheese. Brush the edges with a little water and press together to seal. Brush the tart with the egg and bake for about 20 minutes.

Suggestion. For a change, you can serve this tart instead of the ever-present cheese board. Personally, I'm rather inclined to serve it as a main course with a salad. Great for last-minute dinners, it means I can use up the leftover pieces of cheese lingering in my fridge. Use different dried fruits such as prunes, raisins, walnuts, and filberts. You could also add *prosciutto*.

Apple and orange crumble

Serves 6
Preparation time: 10 minutes
Cooking time: 50 minutes
5 to 6 baking apples
Juice and zest of 1 orange
1 tbsp brown sugar
½ cup sugar
1 cup all-purpose flour
1½ sticks butter

Preheat the oven to 400° F. Slice the apples and sprinkle with the orange juice and zest. Arrange the apple slices in a deep ovenproof dish, and sprinkle with the brown sugar. Put the flour, sugar, and butter in a bowl and work with the fingers until the mixture resembles breadcrumbs. You can also do this with a food processor using the beater attachment. Sprinkle the crumble mixture over the fruits, smooth down lightly, and bake for 50 minutes.

Suggestion. Use acidic fruits such as red berries, plums, pears, rhubarb, or apricots. Add dried fruits and nuts (raisins, prunes, almonds, filberts, or walnuts, etc.). For the crumble mixture you can substitute 1 cup rolled oats or ½ cup whole-wheat flour for ½ cup all-purpose flour. Liven it up by adding spices such as ginger, cinnamon, or nutmeg.

Baked apples with almonds, mascarpone, and honey

Serves 6
Preparation time: 10 minutes
Cooking time: 30 to 40 minutes
6 baking apples
3 tbsp pistachio nuts
3 tbsp finely chopped almonds
3 tbsp finely chopped filberts
½ stick butter
1 lb mascarpone
3 tbsp honey

Preheat the oven to 400° F. Combine the mascarpone with the honey, leaving ripples of honey in the creamy mixture.
Core the apples and fill the cavity with the filberts, almonds, and pistachio nuts.
Top with a knob of butter and bake for 30 to 40 minutes.
Serve without delay, as otherwise the apples deflate. Scrape out the bottom of the dish well, spooning the caramelized juice and butter mixture over the apples. Serve with the mascarpone and honey cream.

Baked figs with rosemary honey

Serves 6
Preparation time: 5 minutes
Cooking time: 15 minutes
A dozen ripe figs
3 or 4 tbsp rosemary (or lavender) honey
1 sprig fresh rosemary (or lavender)

Preheat the oven to 360° F. Rinse and quarter the figs, without opening them up completely. Pull them slightly apart and drizzle a little honey in the center. Bake for 15 minutes. Serve warm with cream cheese, mascarpone, or sour cream. Decorate with a sprig of rosemary or lavender.

Tip. Make this recipe only when figs are in season.

A chocolate fondue

Chocolate fondue

Chocolate fondue

Serves 4
Preparation time: 25 minutes
Cooking time: 5 minutes
7 oz best quality dark chocolate, minimum
60 percent cocoa solids
⅔ cup light cream
¼ stick butter

Prepare a selection of fresh and dried fruits (strawberries, pineapple, kiwi fruit, banana, dried figs, fresh and dried pears, prunes), together with a variety of different cookies (*amaretti*, ladies' fingers, wafer rolls, langues de chat, etc.).
Grate or finely chop the chocolate. Bring the cream and butter almost to boiling point, and pour over the chocolate. Mix together using a whisk and transfer to the fondue bowl.

Tip. You need a special chocolate fondue set for this recipe, or alternatively sit the bowl in a roasting pan of hot water to keep the chocolate at the right temperature.

Nathalie's melt-in-the-mouth gateau

Serves 6 to 8
Preparation time: 5 minutes
Cooking time: 22 minutes
7 oz best quality dark chocolate
1¾ sticks butter
5 eggs
1 tsp all-purpose flour
1¼ cups sugar

Preheat the oven to 375° F. Melt the chocolate and butter in a microwave oven or in a bowl over a pan of hot water. Add the sugar and leave to cool slightly. Add the eggs one by one, stirring with a wooden spoon until each is incorporated. Stir in the flour, then transfer the mixture to a greased cake pan and bake for 22 minutes.
The cake should be only just cooked at the center. Remove from the oven, and turn out immediately onto a wire rack to cool.

Tip. This cake tastes even better if made the evening before, or at least the morning before the dinner party

Nathalie's melt-in-the-mouth gateau

Tanguy

Corentin

Tim

children's
treats

Kids' pizzas in kit form

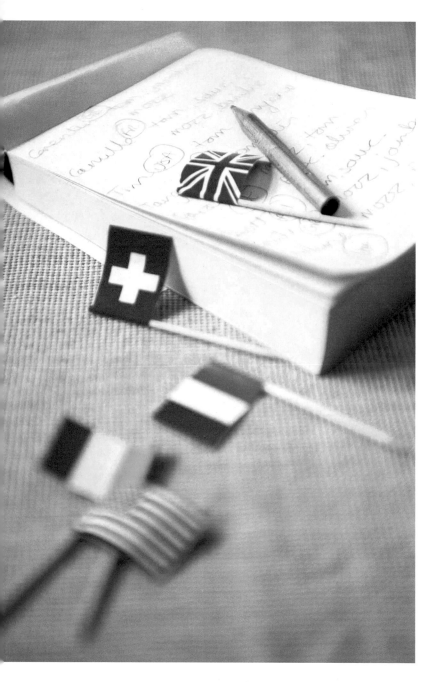

Makes about 8 small pizzas
Preparation time: 30 minutes
Cooking time: 5 minutes
2 portions ready-made pizza dough
8 tbsp finely chopped tomatoes
Sliced tomato, smoked salmon, chopped bacon, mozzarella,
gruyère, eggs, pepperoni, sausage, sour cream, corn, and so on

Preheat the oven to 400° F. Cut out the pizzas and arrange them on big trays. Fill little bowls with all the available toppings and let the children choose, taking their orders as in a restaurant. They'll love it!
Bake for about 5 minutes.

Real fruit drinks

Raspberry, banana, and yogurt flip

Serves 4
Preparation time: 1 minute
7 oz raspberries
2 bananas
1 lb 5 oz yogurt, chilled
6 to 8 ice cubes

Pour all the ingredients into a food processor or blender and blast into a purée. Add more ice cubes if the mixture is too thick.

Orange and cranberry

Serves 4
3¼ cups cranberry juice
Juice of 2 oranges
3 tbsp sugar
4 glasses of crushed ice

Mix together the fruit juices and the sugar, and pour into tall glasses filled with crushed ice. Serve with orange slices and straws.

The citrus drink

Serves 4
Preparation time: 5 minutes
Juice of 2 lemons
Juice of 1 lime
Juice of 4 oranges
4 tbsp sugar
3¼ cups cold water

Combine the fruit juices, water, and sugar, and leave to chill in a refrigerator. Serve with slices of lemon and orange.

Passion fruit, pineapple, and mango

Serves 4
Preparation time: 3 minutes
2 ripe passion fruits
3 cups fresh pineapple juice
1 ripe mango

Blend all the ingredients together in a blender for 1 minute.

Raspberry, banana, and yogurt flip

The citrus drink

Orange and cranberry

Passion fruit, pineapple, and mango

A cake for the boys

Double chocolate chip cookies

Chocolate and almond spread

A cake for the boys

Serves 10
Preparation time: 40 minutes
Cooking time: 25 minutes
Refrigeration time: 1 hour
For the cake
2 sticks unsalted butter, softened
1 cup sugar
5 eggs
2 cups all-purpose flour
1 heaped tsp baking powder
3 to 4 tbsp milk
For the filling (p. 148)
8 oz best quality dark chocolate
1 cup light cream
¼ stick butter
For the decoration
7 oz best quality milk chocolate
1 sheet of acetate (p. 144)
Chocolate caramel toffee sticks

Preheat the oven to 360° F. Grease and flour two 9-inch cake pans. To make the cake, beat together all the ingredients apart from the milk in a food processor for 1 minute until smooth. Reduce the speed, then gradually add the milk. Pour into the 2 cake pans and bake for about 25 minutes.
Leave to cool in the pans for 5 to 10 minutes before turning out onto wire racks to cool completely.
Now make the filling. Heat the cream in a pan and pour over the chocolate. Add the butter and mix together thoroughly using a whisk. Spread the chocolate over one cake, top with the second, then spread over the top of the cake. Leave to set slightly.
Finally, do the decorating. Measure the height and circumference of your cake. Cut out a strip of acetate to match. Place this strip on a second sheet of acetate. Melt the chocolate, then spread on the strip of acetate. When the chocolate has set slightly, but before it hardens completely and become brittle, place the chocolate-covered side of the acetate next to the cake, and press down to coat the cake. This is a delicate operation; an extra pair of hands is always welcome to turn the plate while you wrap it in the chocolate-coated acetate.
Leave to cool completely.
Before serving, remove the strip of acetate, and partially insert the chocolate caramel sticks into the cake. They will gradually absorb moisture and bend in every direction; it's really rather funny.

Tip. I would advise you to do the decorating stage only if you have very good quality milk chocolate and some acetate. If you don't, increase the measurements for the filling by using a third more chocolate, cover the whole cake, including the side, and then insert the chocolate caramel sticks.

Double chocolate chip cookies

Makes about a dozen cookies
Preparation time: 10 minutes
Cooking time: 20 minutes
7 oz chocolate chips
1¾ sticks butter
¾ cup superfine sugar
⅔ cup brown sugar
1 heaped tsp baking powder
2½ cups all-purpose flour
1 egg
7 tbsp cocoa powder

Preheat the oven to 400° F. Beat together the butter and the superfine and brown sugar until pale and fluffy. Add the egg. Sift the flour, baking powder, and cocoa powder together, then add to the mixture, followed by the chocolate chips. Mix well. Using a teaspoon, spoon the mixture into small mounds on a greased baking sheet. Leave plenty of space between them, as they will expand.
Bake for about 10 minutes. Leave to cool on a wire rack.

Tip. It is important not to overcook the cookies if you want them sumptuously soft.

Chocolate and almond spread

Makes 1 large jar
Preparation time: 5 minutes
7 oz best quality dark chocolate
2¾ sticks margarine
18 fl oz sweetened condensed milk
⅔ cup ground almonds or filberts

Ease your conscience by giving your children homemade sweet things. Melt the chocolate in a large bowl in a microwave oven. Add the margarine, then the milk, and finally the ground almonds or hazelnuts. Combine well and keep this spread in an airtight jar in a cool place.

A cake for the girls

Serves 10
Preparation time: 10 minutes
Defrosting time: 30 minutes
3½ pints vanilla ice cream
9 oz pink macaroons (raspberry, rose, or strawberry flavored)

Leave the ice cream to soften for 30 minutes. Meanwhile, crush two-thirds of the macaroons, then incorporate into the softened ice cream. Shape the ice-cream mixture into a small "bombe" and return to the freezer. When ready to serve, decorate with the remaining macaroons and any of the girls' favorite candies that you have to hand.

A cake for the girls

dining
in style

How many dinners have you been to where the hosts spend most of their evening in the kitchen, making only the occasional appearance and barely taking part in the conversation, so preoccupied are they with the meal?

Is it the same with you? The answer is to keep things simple. That doesn't mean tortilla chips with guacamole from the freezer and ice cream every time you invite people over. All it takes is fresh, good quality ingredients. Make a little effort with the presentation, give your menu an original touch with homemade pesto, an exotic spice, or an unusual vegetable, and there you have it! Keeping things simple makes your life easier, so you can spend more time with your guests, without forgetting the tenth vital ingredient of the sauce for the main dish, even after an aperitif of two glasses of champagne followed by a glass of wine with the appetizer.

Here are some of my golden rules:

1
Invite no more than eight guests. If you are cooking for more people (nine or ten), prepare a simple meal or a single dish. If it is a cold meal, don't have too many guests, or you will not have enough room in your refrigerator to keep everything cool.
If the dish needs to be cooked or assembled at the last minute, you will have no chance of joining your guests at the start of the meal.

2
To avoid changing the cutlery and to keep down the number of plates needed, don't serve rolls and butter with the appetizer or the main course. That often spoils people's appetite for the rest of the meal, especially the dessert. It is a good idea to serve a very good cheese at the end of the meal and, finally, some petits-fours (p. 40).

3
Ban anything that might not rise, set, turn out, or reheat at the last minute. Unless you are a culinary wizard that never fails at anything, avoid soufflés, hot and cold mousses, any dishes involving gelatin, white sauces, and zabagliones.

4
If you do want to serve any of these, evaluate them at someone else's house or at a restaurant, and be sure to try out your recipe before serving it to guests.

I don't like cooking dishes that involve pastry parcels (*en papillote*), a salt or pastry crust, a pressure cooker, or any cooking method that prevents me from being able to see how things are progressing until the actual moment of serving. It is too stressful and I need to see if I'm making a mess of things.

5
Always prepare the after-dinner tea and coffee tray before the meal and try to serve little chocolate sweets (p. 154); your guests will feel they have been really pampered.

6
Without entering the realms of folklore, often all it takes to make a dish more appetizing is a little imagination; inventing a name, for example. Why not create a small, personalized menu for the dinner? Your guests will feel that you have been particularly attentive.

7
Make sure that the dining-room lighting does not resemble that of the dentist's office. To create a beautiful effect, place a small, single candle in front of each guest. Provide subdued lighting, but take care that there is enough light. It is irritating if you cannot identify what food is on your plate!

8
If you're dining in style, never accept help from one of your guests; that can only impair your concentration in the kitchen. I want to see if my dishes are going wrong, but I don't want to show them to other people before I've been able to remedy the damage!

Many of my most interesting dishes are nothing more than cleverly disguised mistakes.

Sophisticated cream soups

Cream of leek soup with oysters

Cream of mushroom soup with smoked salmon

Cream of shrimp and star anise soup

Cream of leek soup with oysters

Serves 6
Preparation time: 10 minutes
Cooking time: 30 minutes
18 oysters
6 leeks, sliced
½ stick butter
4 cups vegetable stock (p. 180)
2 cups water
1¼ cups light cream
2 large potatoes, diced
Salt and pepper

In a large pan, sweat the leeks and potatoes in the butter. Add the water and stock, season lightly with salt and pepper, and cook over low heat for 20 to 25 minutes. Blend in a blender until very smooth, then add the cream. Place 3 oysters (shells removed!) in the bottom of each bowl and pour over the cream soup, which will poach the oysters.

Suggestion. Try the oysters with the cream of cèpe mushrooms and truffle soup (p. 60), it's equally delicious!

Cream of mushroom soup with smoked salmon

Serves 6
Preparation time: 15 minutes
Cooking time: 20 minutes
1 lb mushrooms (a mixture of chanterelles, if you can get them, and small mushrooms)
2 shallots
4 cups vegetable stock (p. 180)
¼ stick butter
1⅔ cups light cream
6 tbsp diced smoked salmon
Salt and pepper
Chervil

Brush the mushrooms clean and quickly rinse under cold running water if necessary. In a pan, sweat the shallots in the butter and add the mushrooms. Cook gently for a few minutes until the mushrooms have released their juices. Add the stock and simmer for 10 to 15 minutes. Blend in a blender and pour in the cream, then season to taste. When ready to serve, place the diced salmon in the bottom of the bowls and pour over the cream soup. Garnish with the chopped chervil.

Tip. Diced salmon is sometimes sold in vacuum packs. If you cannot find any, buy slices instead and cut them into strips.

Cream of shrimp and star anise soup

Serves 4
Preparation time: 30 minutes
Cooking time: 25 minutes
2lb 4 oz fresh shrimp
2 cups white wine
4 cups water
1 cup light cream
2 star anise
½ leek
1 carrot
2 shallots
Salt and pepper

Cook the shrimp in boiling water seasoned with salt and pepper and 1 star anise for 3 to 4 minutes.
Drain and leave to cool so that you do not scald your fingers when shelling the shrimp tails. Set the tails aside.
Cook the shrimp heads with the water, wine, finely chopped vegetables, and the remaining star anise for 20 minutes. You need to make 4 cups of stock, in which you will gently reheat the shrimp tails. Whizz in a blender until very smooth, then add the cream.
Do not allow to boil. Season to taste and serve immediately.

Chilled cucumber soup

Serves 6
Preparation time: 25 minutes
Refrigeration time: 2 hours
3 cucumbers
Juice of 1 lemon
1¼ cups light cream
4 small containers of yogurt
1 small container of mascarpone
1 tbsp finely chopped mint
1 tbsp finely chopped basil
Olive oil
Salt and pepper

Peel the cucumbers, remove the seeds, then blend until very smooth. Add the cream, yogurt, and lemon juice. Combine the herbs with the mascarpone and season to taste. When ready to serve, pour the soup into bowls, place a spoonful of the mascarpone mixture on top, and drizzle with olive oil.

Chilled cucumber soup

Scallops with a difference

Scallops marinated in olive oil

Scallops roasted in butter

Cream of carrot, cumin, and scallop soup

Scallops marinated in olive oil

Serves 4
Preparation time: 15 minutes
Marinating time: 1 hour
8 to 10 fresh scallops
2 tbsp lemon juice
6 tbsp extra virgin olive oil
2 tbsp finely chopped fresh basil
2 tbsp pine nuts
Sea salt

Finely slice the scallops. Arrange like the petals of a flower on the plates, and brush with a mixture of the lemon juice and the oil. Custom has it that you should not serve the coral-colored parts, but this is purely a matter of taste. Personally, I use them, because they add a dash of color to an otherwise bland-looking dish. Cut them across into two or three pieces, and alternate with the slices of white flesh. Cover with plastic wrap and place in a refrigerator. When ready to serve, sprinkle with the basil, pine nuts, and a pinch of sea salt.

Tip. Nowadays, you can find countless top quality oils in supermarkets or delicatessens. Pine nut oil would be ideal for this recipe, if you can find it.

Scallops roasted in butter

Serves 4
Cooking time: 15 minutes
12 large scallops, cleaned
1 stick butter, finely diced
Sea salt and pepper

Place 3 scallops in each individual casserole dish. Sprinkle with the butter, season, and roast for 2 to 5 minutes in an oven preheated to 400° F. Serve immediately.

Cream of carrot, cumin, and scallop soup

Serves 6
Preparation time: 10 minutes
Cooking time: 25 minutes
12 carrots, sliced
½ stick butter
1 tbsp olive oil
4 cups vegetable stock (p. 180)
2 cups water
3 to 4 tbsp sour cream
1 tbsp ground cumin
6 large scallops
Sea salt
Pepper

In a pan, heat the oil and butter, brown the carrots for a few minutes, then add the water and stock. Cook over low heat for 20 to 25 minutes. Blend until smooth, then add the cumin, some salt and pepper, and the cream.
Keep hot. Quickly broil the scallops. Place a scallop in each bowl and pour over the hot soup.

Scallops with chestnuts

Serves 4
Preparation time: 10 minutes
Cooking time: 15 minutes
12 large scallops with coral-colored parts
3 shallots
¼ stick butter
1 tbsp oil
About 15 chestnuts
4 tbsp diced bacon
1¼ cups light cream
Salt and pepper

Heat the butter and oil in a skillet. Fry the shallots, diced bacon, and chestnuts until golden, then add the cream and the coral-colored parts of the scallops. Cook for 1 minute, pressing the corals down with a spoon or spatula. In another skillet or on a very hot griddle, brown the scallops, then add them to the sauce to cook through. Season to taste and serve immediately.

Scallops with chestnuts

Fresh market vegetables

Salad of crispy vegetables

Cucumber, olive, and avocado tartare with *raïta*

Mini zucchini with a double tomato stuffing

Salad of crispy vegetables

Serves 4 to 6
Preparation time: 10 minutes
Cooking time: 15 minutes
1 lb 12 oz fresh vegetables (peas, carrots, green beans,
sugar snap peas, baby corn, etc.)
5 tbsp olive oil
1 tbsp sesame oil
2 tbsp sesame seeds
1 tbsp soy sauce

Steam each vegetable separately so they are very crisp. Combine
the two oils and the soy sauce to make a dressing. Arrange the
vegetables attractively, pour over the dressing, sprinkle with the
sesame seeds, and serve.

Tip. Use the early vegetables and baby vegetables that are
beginning to appear in almost all supermarkets.

Cucumber, olive, and avocado tartare with raïta

Serves 4
Preparation time: 25 minutes
1 cucumber
1 tbsp black olives
1 tbsp green olives
1 avocado
2 tbsp olive oil
Juice of 1 lemon
3 small containers of Greek yogurt, or whole-milk yogurt
1 tbsp dill
1 tbsp mint
1 tbsp chives
1 tsp tarragon
Salt and pepper

If possible, combine the herbs with the yogurt a few hours before
serving, to allow their flavors to develop. Beat the olive oil with the
lemon juice. Peel and seed the cucumber and peel the avocado.
Finely dice the cucumber, olives, and avocado. Combine these
ingredients together with a tablespoon of the oil-and-lemon
sauce. Set aside in a refrigerator.
Just before serving, combine the remaining dressing with the
yogurt sauce, and season with salt and pepper. Using a stainless
steel ring or glass approximately 2½ inches in diameter, shape the
tartare mixture into mounds in the center of the plates, and pour
the raïta around and over them.

Tip. If you are short of time, you can cut the vegetables into
larger pieces, put them in a single large dish, and serve the raïta
separately.

Mini zucchini with double tomato stuffing

Serves 4
Preparation time: 20 minutes
Cooking time: 15 minutes
4 small, round zucchini
3 to 4 large ripe tomatoes
3 to 4 slices of sun-dried tomato
2 tbsp chopped cilantro
2 tsp chopped basil
Olive oil
Salt and pepper

Using a shaped paring knife (p. 160), cut zigzag shapes into the
zucchini, without removing any pieces. Steam the zucchini for
12 to 15 minutes. Scrape out the seeds from the zucchini using a
tomato scoop (p. 160), and leave to cool.
Chop the fresh and dried tomatoes, conserving the juice, and mix
together. Combine with the herbs, salt, pepper, and olive oil, and
spoon into the zucchini. Arrange any excess filling around the
zucchini. You can prepare this recipe 2 to 3 hours in advance.

Tip. Serve with Parmesan crisps. Preheat the oven to 360° F. Using
a stainless steel ring or glass, make rounds of grated Parmesan on
a baking sheet, and bake for 3 to 4 minutes until golden. Remove
from the oven and curl into crisps before they cool and become
brittle.

Asparagus with Parmesan

Serves 4 to 6
Preparation time: 5 minutes
Cooking time: 15 minutes
2 bundles of green asparagus
5 tbsp olive oil
2 tbsp balsamic vinegar
100 g (4 oz) fresh Parmesan
Salt and pepper

Wash the asparagus, trim the ends, and steam for about 10 to
12 minutes. Make a dressing using the oil, vinegar, salt, and
pepper.
Pour the dressing over the asparagus tips and scatter with large
flakes of Parmesan made with a paring knife.

Asparagus with Parmesan

Spring vegetables with savory spiced butter

Asparagus with poached eggs

Hot appetizers

Spring vegetables with savory spiced butter

Serves 4 to 6
Preparation time: 10 minutes
Butter preparation time: 1 hour (p. 172)
Cooking time: 20 minutes
1 lb 5 oz to 1 lb 12 oz) spring vegetables
(turnips, carrots, peas, asparagus, etc.), peeled
4 to 5 oz savory spiced butter (p. 172)

If possible, steam the vegetables separately. Alternatively, boil them separately in salted water. They must still be crisp. Take care, as peas cook in just 1 or 2 minutes. Set aside and keep warm. When ready to serve, arrange the vegetables on each plate and top with a generous knob of savory spiced butter.

Asparagus with poached eggs

Serves 4 to 6
Preparation time: 10 minutes
Cooking time: 20 minutes
2 bundles of green asparagus
4 to 6 very fresh eggs
Wine vinegar
Salt and pepper

Clean and trim the asparagus, then steam for 12 to 15 minutes. Break the eggs and poach them in simmering water with a little wine vinegar. Arrange a few asparagus spears on each plate, place an egg on top, season to taste, and serve immediately.

Crushed smooth-skinned potatoes with a Munster and caraway coulis

Serves 6
Preparation time: 30 minutes
Cooking time: 20 minutes
About 15 waxy new potatoes
14 oz Munster cheese (or Camembert)
2 tbsp light cream
2 tbsp caraway or cumin seeds

Steam or boil the potatoes for about 20 minutes.
You can peel them if you really find the skin offensive—although perhaps not the tiny ones!
Remove the rind of the cheese, and melt the cheese gently in a pan together with the cream. Crush the potatoes, divide between six small plates or place in one large bowl, and pour the melted cheese over the top. Sprinkle with the caraway or cumin seeds and serve immediately with pickled gherkins or any other pickles.

Crushed smooth-skinned potatoes with a Munster and caraway coulis

Ostrich steak in a tomato and almond crust

Buffalo steak with caramelized beets

To make a change from beef

Ostrich steak in a tomato and almond crust

Serves 4
Preparation time: 10 minutes
Cooking time: 15 minutes
4 ostrich steaks, each weighing about 5 to 7 oz
4 tbsp puréed sun-dried tomatoes
4 tbsp chopped almonds
Salt and pepper

Preheat the oven to 430° F. Combine the tomato purée with the almonds and spread on top of the steaks. Season with salt and pepper. Bake for about 12 to 15 minutes. Serve with a crispy green salad.

Buffalo steak with caramelized beets

Serves 4
Cooking time: 5 to 8 minutes
4 buffalo steaks, each weighing about 5 oz
2 pieces of cooked beets, cut into chip-shaped pieces
4 tbsp sugar
2 tbsp olive oil
A few juniper berries
Salt and pepper

Heat a griddle pan to a high temperature for the meat and a skillet with the olive oil for the beets. Brown the meat and fry the beets for 2 or 3 minutes.
Sprinkle with the sugar, and leave to caramelize. Serve the steaks and beets drizzled with the cooking juices. Season with salt and pepper, and place juniper berries on top.

Rabbit with Gorgonzola

Serves 6
Cooking time: 40 minutes
6 saddles of rabbit
7 oz Gorgonzola cheese
2 cups wine
2 shallots, finely chopped
¼ stick butter
1 tbsp all-purpose flour
1 tbsp olive oil
1 cup light cream
Salt and pepper

Heat the oil and butter in a casserole dish and brown the shallots and the saddles of rabbit. Sprinkle with the flour and cook for 1 minute until all the fat has been absorbed.
Add the wine and a little water and cook over low heat for about 35 minutes. Add the Gorgonzola to the sauce and stir until melted. Add the cream, season to taste, and serve with pasta.

Tip. Remove the fatty bits on the sides of the saddles before cooking to prevent the sauce from being gelatinous.

Rabbit with Gorgonzola

Mussel and lobster ragout

Serves 6
Preparation time: 40 minutes
Cooking time: 20 minutes
3 lobsters, each weighing approximately 1 lb 5 oz
5 pints mussels
2 shallots
1 tbsp olive oil
1¼ cups white wine
1 cup light cream
½ tsp ground cumin
1 large pinch of saffron threads
Salt and pepper

Bring a large stockpot of water to boiling point. Season with salt and pepper and cook the lobsters for about 10 minutes. Drain, and leave to cool. Shell the lobster, and set aside the flesh in a bowl. Cover with plastic wrap. Clean the mussels. Sweat the shallots for a few minutes in olive oil, add the wine, and bring to boiling point. Add the mussels, shake well, and cook over high heat for 3 to 4 minutes. Drain, collecting the juices in another pan, then shell the mussels, discarding any that have not opened. Set aside with the lobster. Boil the liquid for a few minutes until it is slightly reduced. Add the cream, saffron, cumin, salt, and pepper. Cut the lobster into pieces and add, together with the mussels, to the sauce. Cook over low heat until they have heated through, then serve immediately.

Tip. Use Maine lobster unless you prefer another type. The mussels, however, must be fresh, not frozen.

Mussel and lobster ragout

At the fish market

Fried sea bass with a warm salad dressing

Cod with red pesto

Tuna steak with salsa

Fried sea bass with a warm salad dressing

Serves 4
Preparation time for the tomatoes: 2 hours in advance
Cooking time: 5 minutes for the fish
4 sea bass fillets, each weighing about 7 oz, skin on
8 small, ripe Italian tomatoes
4 handfuls of arugula
4 to 5 tbsp olive oil
2 tbsp balsamic vinegar dressing
Sea salt and white pepper

Prepare the conserved tomatoes (p. 176) and the balsamic vinegar dressing (p. 178). In a skillet fry the sea bass fillets in the very hot olive oil for 2 to 3 minutes. Gently heat the dressing in a microwave oven or in a pan. Meanwhile, place a handful of arugula on each plate together with 4 tomato halves. Place the fish fillets on top, skin side up, and pour over a little of the dressing. Season with salt and pepper and serve immediately.

Cod with red pesto

Serves 4
Preparation time: 10 minutes
Cooking time: 3 to 4 minutes for the fish; the mash: 25 minutes (p. 170)
1 lb 5 oz to 1 lb 12 oz cod
2 tbsp red pesto (p. 174)
8 slices of sun-dried tomato
Olive oil
Butter
4 large sprigs of basil to garnish

Make the olive oil mashed potatoes. Steam or microwave the cod for 3 to 4 minutes in a covered dish with a little water and butter. Thin the pesto down a little with the olive oil. When ready to serve, place the hot potatoes, tomato slices, and cod in layers one on top of the other. Use a stainless steel ring (p. 160) to make the layers even. Garnish with the pesto and basil.

Tuna steak with salsa

Serves 4
Preparation time: 15 minutes
Cooking time: 4 minutes
4 slices of tuna, each weighing about 6 oz
6 firm tomatoes, skinned, seeded, and diced
2 shallots, finely chopped
1 red bell pepper, diced
2 tsp parsley
1 small red chile (optional), finely chopped
Chinese chili sauce (optional)
Salt and pepper

Mix together the tomatoes, shallots, chile pepper, if using, and red bell pepper to make the salsa. Add the parsley, salt, and pepper.
Broil the fish on a barbecue or on a very hot griddle. Serve immediately with the salsa.

Tip. Take care if using a chile pepper, because it is very strong. A large green or red chile pepper will be less strong than its little brother. To make it less strong, you can leave it to soak in a bowl of cold water for about ½ hour before cooking it whole.

If you are using it sliced, remove the seeds and the inner membrane and use the pointed end of the chile pepper. Watch out for stinging fingers! A salsa containing chile will always cause a stir.

Salmon with lime and ginger

Serves 4
Cooking time: 10 minutes
4 salmon steaks, each weighing about 7 oz
1 tbsp finely chopped fresh ginger
Juice and zest of 1 lime
½ stick butter
2 tbsp sour cream
Salt and pepper

Cut the lime zest into julienne strips and blanch in boiling water for 1 minute. Heat the lime juice and ginger over low heat for 2 minutes. Beat in the butter and set aside.
Steam the salmon for 3 to 4 minutes; it should be only just cooked inside. Add the sour cream to the sauce, season, and reheat gently. Coat the fish in the sauce and garnish with the lime zest julienne strips. Serve with Chinese or Japanese noodles.

Salmon with lime and ginger

A bit richer

Conserve of duck with caramelized garlic and shallots

Parmentier of black pudding with filberts

Pan-fried fresh foie gras with balsamic caramel sauce

Confit of duck with caramelized garlic and shallots

Serves 4
Preparation time: 10 minutes
Cooking time: 30 minutes
3 duck thighs preserved in their own fat
4 or 5 large potatoes
¼ stick butter
1 cup milk
3 garlic cloves
6 shallots
2 tbsp olive oil
1 tbsp sugar

Use the potatoes, butter, and milk to make mashed potato (p. 170). Brown the garlic and shallots in the oil for 3 minutes. Add the sugar and caramelize by continuing to cook for a further 2 minutes. Reheat the conserved duck thighs in a microwave oven or in a casserole. Remove the bones and slice the meat thinly. Proceed as for the black pudding (see below); make up in layers, finishing with the caramelized garlic and shallots.

Parmentier of black pudding with filberts

Serves 4
Preparation time: 15 minutes
Cooking time: 30 minutes
12 oz black pudding (blood sausage)
4 or 5 large potatoes
3 ripe pears
¼ stick butter
1 cup milk
6 tbsp chopped or finely chopped filberts

Use the potatoes, butter, milk, and pear to make mashed potato (p. 170). Fry the black pudding for about 5 minutes. Remove the skin and set the sausage meat aside, keeping it hot.
Using a stainless steel ring, make up alternate layers of mash and black pudding. Garnish with the filberts and serve.

Pan-fried fresh foie gras with a balsamic caramel sauce

Serves 6
Cooking time: 7 minutes
6 slices of fresh foie gras, ¾ inch thick
4 tbsp superfine sugar
4 tbsp balsamic vinegar
Sea salt
White pepper

To make the caramel sauce, pour the sugar and vinegar in a casserole and cook over high heat. Stir for 5 minutes. Remove from the heat and set aside.
In a very hot skillet, brown the foie gras for 1 minute on each side. Transfer to warmed plates and coat with the caramel sauce. Sprinkle with sea salt and white pepper. Serve with crunchy steamed baby turnips.

Tip. When frying the foie gras, open your window wide, or switch your oven hood on full. Remember to protect yourself from the spitting fat by donning an apron.
If you buy cheap foie gras, coat the liver slices in flour before frying; cheap foie gras produces a lot more fat and water than better quality foie gras.
If you don't manage to make the caramel sauce, just leave it out! Discard the fat and deglaze the skillet with the vinegar. Another option is to make a warm balsamic vinegar dressing (p. 178) and pour it over the liver.

Capon with morels

Serves 6
Cooking time: 1 hour
Soaking time: 2 hours for the morels
1 capon or chicken weighing about 4 lbs, cut into pieces
2 oz dried morels
½ stick butter
2 shallots
1½ cups dry white wine
1⅝ cups light cream
Salt and pepper

Leave the morels to soak in hot water, adding a dash of Armagnac if you like. Fry the capon pieces in half of the butter until golden. Add the shallots and wine. Season with salt and pepper, cover, and simmer for about 30 minutes.
Drain the morels well, brown them in a skillet with the remaining butter for 5 to 6 minutes, stirring constantly, then spoon them over the capon pieces. Cook for a further 10 minutes. Add the cream and serve hot with a mixture of ordinary and wild rice.

Capon with morels

Double cheese and black bread terrine

Serves 6 to 8
Preparation time: 25 minutes
Assembly time: 20 minutes
Refrigeration time: 1 to 2 hours
4 slices of black (rye) bread
8 oz Camembert, rind removed
8 oz Roquefort
2 sticks butter
1 cup chopped filberts
1 cup raisins

In the bowl of a food processor, blend together half the butter
with the Roquefort, then add the filberts. Proceed in the same
way to make a similar mixture with the Camembert, raisins, and
the remaining butter.

Line a loaf pan with plastic wrap.
Cut up the black bread and use to line the base of the pan.
Spread a layer of the Roquefort mixture on the bread base.
Add a second layer of bread, then spread with the Camembert
mixture. The loaf pan will be only a third or half full, but that will be
sufficient for the number of guests indicated. Chill in a refrigerator
for 1 to 2 hours.

Before serving, turn out and cut into thin slices, and serve with a
salad.

Tip. This terrine is always a great success.
You can make it the evening before, but do not slice it until just
before serving. If there are more of you, just add a third layer!

Other combinations are possible: Munster cheese with cumin or
caraway seeds or even Gorgonzola with dried apricots or prunes.

Spiced dried and soft winter fruit compote

Light fruit gratin

Spiced dried and soft winter fruit compote

Serves 6
Preparation time: 15 minutes
Cooking time: 20 minutes
3 cooking apples, cut into quarters
2 pears, cut into quarters
1 orange, sliced
1 banana, sliced
1 fresh pineapple, cut into chunks
Juice of 1 lemon
6 dried apricots
6 prunes
6 dried figs
4 cloves
1 tsp cardamom seeds
1 tsp nutmeg
1 vanilla bean, split lengthwise
2 glasses of orange juice (preferably freshly squeezed)
2 cups water

Place the apples in a pan, and add the orange juice and water. Add the spices and cook slowly, adding the other fruits in stages. Simmer very gently for 20 minutes—the apples should be very soft. Add water if necessary. Leave to cool and serve in an attractive glass bowl.

Light fruit gratin

Serves 4 to 6
Preparation time: 25 minutes
Cooking time: 3 minutes
½ cup sugar
4 eggs, separated
1 cup whole milk
1 cup light cream
1 vanilla bean
1 tbsp all-purpose flour
6 tbsp fruit (mango, raspberries, strawberries, figs, etc.)

To make the confectioner's custard, beat the egg yolks with the sugar and flour until the mixture is pale and frothy. Meanwhile, bring the milk and cream to boiling point with the split vanilla bean. Pour over the egg-and-sugar mixture and cook for 1 minute, stirring constantly. Just before serving, remove the vanilla bean, whisk the egg whites into peaks and fold into the confectioner's custard. Arrange the fruits in a small gratin dish, cover with the egg mixture, and grill for 2 or 3 minutes until golden, watching carefully. Serve immediately.

Tip. You can prepare the confectioner's custard and the fruits before the meal and whisk the whites at the last minute. Do not put the fruits or the cream mixture in the refrigerator. The latter will congeal, making it difficult to fold in the egg whites; as for the fruits, they will be too cold.

Fruit sushis

Serves 6
Preparation time: 15 minutes
Cooking time: 40 minutes
Refrigeration time: 1 hour
Assembly time: 5 to 20 minutes
1 cup rice
3 cups whole milk
1 vanilla bean, split
½ cup sugar
1 kiwi fruit
3 or 4 strawberries
1 fresh fig
1 peach or nectarine
1 slice of melon
Mint leaves
6 pitted prunes
6 tbsp maple syrup
4 tbsp apricot jam

Wash the rice. Boil it in a large pan of water for about 5 minutes. Drain. Place the rice, milk, and vanilla bean in a pan and cook over low heat until all the liquid has been absorbed (30 to 35 minutes). When the rice is cooked, add the sugar, and leave to cool completely. Cut all the fruits except the prunes into very thin slices. Spoon a little of the rice mixture into the prunes. Make the rest of the rice into sushi-shaped rolls and decorate with the strips of fruit and mint leaves. Coat with the warmed apricot jam. Serve with the maple syrup.

Fruit sushis

Chocolate mille-feuilles with candied clementine zest

Petits pots de chocolat

Double chocolate tart

Chocolate mille-feuilles with candied clementine zest

Serves 4
Preparation time: 20 minutes
Cooking time: 25 minutes for the syrup
Refrigeration time: 1 hour
7 oz best quality dark chocolate
⅔ cup whipping cream
1 tbsp clementine syrup
Zest of 3 clementines
For the syrup
2 cups water
1¼ cups sugar
Zest of 2 oranges
1 tbsp orange liqueur (optional)

Melt the chocolate in a microwave oven or in a bowl over hot water. Using a 3–4 inch stainless steel ring, make very thin disks of chocolate on a sheet of acetate (p. 144) or waxed paper, and leave to cool. Whip the cream and add the clementine syrup and clementine zest. Assemble the mille-feuille by alternating 3 or 4 disks of chocolate with a spoonful of cream.
To make the syrup, gently heat the water, orange zest, and sugar in a pan for about 20 minutes until the sugar has dissolved. Leave to cool. When ready to serve, drizzle the syrup over the mille-feuilles.

Tip. To make life simpler, decorate the mille-feuilles with very fine strips of candied orange instead of the syrup. You could also add the orange liqueur to the syrup.

Petits pots de chocolat

Serves 6 to 8
Cooking time: 10 minutes
Refrigeration time: 2 hours
1⅔ cups whipping cream
9 oz best quality dark bitter chocolate, chopped or in drops
4 very fresh egg yolks
¼ stick butter, melted

Bring the cream almost to boiling point and pour over the chocolate drops or grated or chopped chocolate. Stir until smooth. Beat the egg yolks and add to the chocolate cream mixture. Pour in the melted butter. Stir well and spoon into little pots. Leave to cool completely in a refrigerator, taking them out 20 minutes before serving.

Double chocolate tart

Serves 6 to 8
Preparation time: 20 minutes
Cooking time: 35 minutes
Refrigeration time: 2 hours
1 quantity sweet chocolate pastry (p. 182)
2 eggs and 3 egg yolks
2½ tbsp sugar
7 oz dark chocolate, chopped or in drops
1¼ sticks butter

Preheat the oven to 360° F and bake the pastry shell blind for 15 to 20 minutes. Remove from the oven and leave to cool completely. Leave the oven on. Beat the eggs, egg yolks, and sugar until pale and fluffy. Melt the chocolate drops or chopped chocolate with the butter, stirring until very smooth.
Leave to cool slightly, then add the egg mixture and beat rapidly until smooth. Fill the tart shell and bake for 5 minutes. Leave to cool, then serve.

Virginie's chocolate pavé

Serves 6
Preparation time: 40 minutes
Refrigeration time: 5 to 6 hours
14 oz best quality bitter chocolate
1 stick butter
4 egg yolks
⅔ cup confectioners' sugar
2 cups heavy cream, whipped

Melt the chocolate with the butter in a microwave oven or in a bowl over hot water. Beat the egg yolks with the sugar until the mixture becomes pale. Combine the two mixtures, beating with a whisk, then add the whipped cream. Transfer the mixture to a loaf pan lined with plastic wrap. Leave to chill in a refrigerator for 5 to 6 hours.

Tip. Use the new molds that do not need to be lined or greased and which turn things out as though by magic. For a more stylish presentation, you could pour some melted cooking chocolate onto a sheet of acetate or waxed paper, sprinkle with slivered chocolate, cocoa beans and cocoa powder, then leave to cool completely (30 minutes to 1 hour depending on the room temperature), before peeling off.
This may never be as good as Virginie's, but you can try to make it in the hope that one day she'll invite you to taste the real thing!

Virginie's chocolate pavé

homemade
chocolates

Chocolate, how to use it

The quality of chocolate does not depend solely on its cocoa content; chocolate with 72 percent cocoa solids content will not necessarily be better than chocolate with only 60 percent. A high percentage can sometimes result in a dusty taste and a certain acidity instead of the much sought-after bitterness.

Chocolates must be strong, round, and tasty, and must linger on the palate. Let's not denigrate milk and white chocolate. Milk blends wonderfully with many flavors, such as vanilla, caramel, or cinnamon; white chocolate adds flavor and creaminess to countless desserts and mousses.

No matter whether it is dark, milk, or white, "*couverture*" is the king of chocolate, used by professional chocolate-makers, pastry chefs, and chefs. The selection of whole cocoa beans and the way they are processed to produce a finished product—the important presence of cocoa butter—make it smoother, more creamy, more melt-in-the-mouth, easier to work with, and clearly superior to other types of chocolate, such as "eating," "cooking," or "sweet."

Couverture chocolate is more expensive because of its high cocoa butter content. You can buy it in some specialist shops, in some good delicatessens, or even by mail order (p. 192).

If you can't find *couverture*, just buy the very best chocolate your supermarket or delicatessen has to offer, but you will always be aware of the difference, both in its flavor and in the ease with which you are able to make your creations.

Tempering

Tempering chocolate is a technique that helps it retain its gloss and avoid white traces of cocoa butter when molding. The flavor is the same whether or not the chocolate is tempered.

When you buy a block, it is glossy. If you want it to retain its gloss and hardness after molding, you must heat it, cool it again, and then reheat it to be able to work with it.

The easiest and quickest method is the "two thirds/one third" method. It is best to use chocolate drops for this method. Armed with a cooking thermometer, heat two thirds of the chocolate in a microwave oven or in a bowl over hot water to a temperature approaching 113° F. It is important not to add any water or milk. Stir carefully and add the remaining third of the chocolate. This will cause the temperature to drop rapidly.

Stir until the chocolate drops have melted completely, then reheat to about 86° F, at which temperature it is possible to work the chocolate.

If you have managed to get hold of *couverture* chocolate, the temperature curves to be observed will be stated in the instructions.

If all that seems a bit complicated, and it usually does, then remember that people train long and hard to become master chocolate-makers or pastry chefs—it's not something that happens overnight. But with the right equipment and ingredients, you will have no difficulty following these recipes.

If you are cooking for a special occasion or for a very stylish dinner, you need a dessert that will rise to the occasion. So you need have no qualms about running to your local chocolate or cake store to order a box of real chocolates or a cake that looks out of this world.

The right tools for the professional chocolate-maker. YOU CAN ALWAYS TRY TO IMPROVISE WITH VARIOUS OBJECTS, BUT ONCE YOU HAVE USED THESE TOOLS, YOU WON'T BE ABLE TO MANAGE WITHOUT THEM!

1 Curved sheet or half pipe to make *tuiles* (wafer-thin cookies): this device takes the place of the rolling pin or bottle when it comes to making *tuiles*. Use it to take the stress out of chocolate-making!

2 Special plastic acetate: it helps make the chocolate glossy and allows it to harden. It is excellent for creating original shapes and decorations and makes it easy to turn out any chocolate creation from its mold. It also protects work surfaces. It's magic!

3 Triangular spatula and angled spatula: the triangle lifts off the set chocolate with ease and is useful for making shavings and creating fan shapes on chocolate before it has fully hardened. The angled spatula is perfect for smoothing the chocolate out when using it for molds or glazing.

4 Dipping forks: small tools specially designed to make it easier to coat individual candies, dried fruits, almond paste, and so on. So much more practical than an ordinary fork!

5 Presentation boxes: why not get some real chocolate presentation boxes to make an impressive gift of your homemade chocolates?

1

2

3

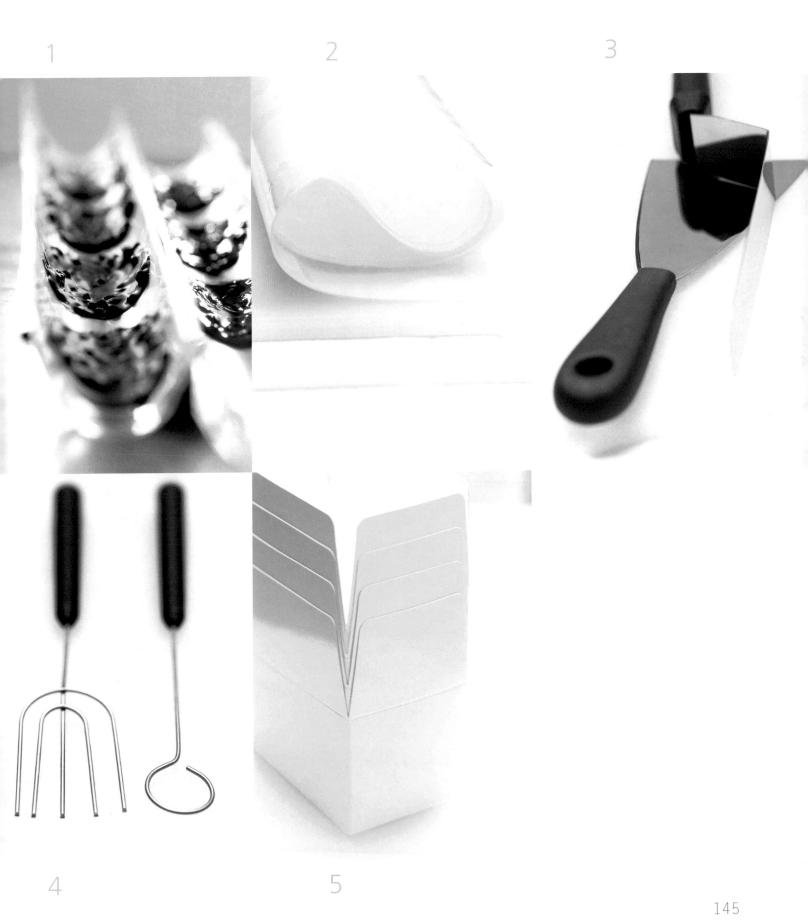

4

5

Ganaches: vanilla milk chocolate, pure dark chocolate, and dark chocolate with orange and cardamom

Truffles

Ganache chocolates and truffles

GANACHE IS A MIXTURE OF CHOCOLATE AND CREAM, MORE OR LESS CREAM BEING ADDED DEPENDING ON THE CONSISTENCY DESIRED. FOR TRUFFLES, THE PROPORTION IN WEIGHT IS ROUGHLY TWO QUANTITIES OF CHOCOLATE TO ONE OF CREAM. FOR A SMOOTHER TEXTURE, YOU CAN ALSO ADD BUTTER OR GLUCOSE. IF WHIPPED UP WITH AN ELECTRIC MIXER, GANACHE BECOMES MORE MOUSSE-LIKE AND MAKES AN EXCELLENT CAKE FILLING. IT CAN BE FLAVORED, SHAPED, AND WRAPPED IN DECORATIVE PAPER TO MAKE A WIDE VARIETY OF CHOCOLATES.

Pure dark chocolate

Serves 8
Preparation time: 5 minutes
Refrigeration time: 2 hours
4 oz best quality very bitter chocolate, either drops,
or grated or broken up into pieces
3½–4 tbsp whipping cream

Bring the cream almost to boiling point and pour over the chocolate. Stir gently with a spoon until smooth. Pour into a container.

Dark chocolate with orange and cardamom

Serves 8
Preparation time: 5 minutes
Refrigeration time: 2 hours
4 oz best quality dark orange-flavored chocolate
or 2 oz best quality dark chocolate, minimum 60 percent
cocoa solids and ½ spoonful grated orange zest
A small pinch of crushed cardamom seeds
3½–4 tbsp whipping cream

Proceed as for the first recipe, adding the grated zest and the cardamom seeds to the chocolate-cream mixture. Store in a refrigerator.

Vanilla milk chocolate

Serves 8
Preparation time: 5 minutes
Refrigeration time: 2 hours
4 oz best quality milk chocolate
1 vanilla bean
3½–4 tbsp whipping cream

Split the vanilla bean in half, place in a pan with the cream, and heat. Leave to infuse, scraping the vanilla bean to extract all the seeds. Pour over the chocolate, stir well, and pour into containers.

Truffles

Makes about 30 to 40 truffles
Preparation time: 5 minutes
Refrigeration time: 2 hours
For the ganache
1 lb best quality chocolate
1 cup whipping cream

Make a ganache as explained in the heading above and leave to cool. Shape into small balls and coat with white and dark chocolate, cocoa powder, slivered cocoa beans, toasted and finely chopped almonds, or filberts.

Truffles

Mendiants

Chocolate-coated dried fruits

Rochers

Tuiles

Mendiants

Makes about 25
Preparation time: 30 minutes
4 oz best quality dark chocolate
1 tbsp green pistachio nuts
¼ cup golden raisins
¼ cup blanched almonds
2 oz strips of candied orange peel
A sheet of acetate (p. 144) or a sheet of waxed paper

Place a sheet of acetate or waxed paper on a marble slab or other smooth, cold surface. Melt the chocolate in a microwave oven or in a bowl over hot water. Place a scant teaspoonful of melted chocolate on the sheet and shape into a disk using the back of a spoon. Make several at a time so that the chocolate does not become too cool. Place a golden raisin, pistachio, almond, and halved strip of orange on each disk, and leave to cool completely. The *mendiants* are ready when they come off the acetate or waxed paper with ease.

Chocolate-coated dried fruits

Makes 1 lb
Preparation time: 25 minutes
Refrigeration time: 30 minutes to 1 hour
9 oz best quality chocolate
7 oz dried fruits (apricots, prunes, dates, figs, pears, etc.)
A sheet of acetate (p. 144) or a sheet of waxed paper

Melt the chocolate in a microwave oven or in a bowl over hot water. Drop the fruits into the chocolate one by one, ensure they are coated perfectly, then remove them using 2 forks or—better still—a professional chocolate-maker's dipping fork (p. 144), allowing any excess chocolate to drip back into the bowl. Leave the fruits to set at room temperature on a sheet of acetate or waxed paper.

Rochers

Makes about 20
Preparation time: 40 minutes
4 oz slivered almonds
2 tbsp sugar syrup
1 tbsp confectioners' sugar
5 oz best quality dark or milk chocolate

Preheat the oven to 360° F. Combine the almonds with the sugar syrup and shape into small mounds on a nonstick baking sheet. Sprinkle with the confectioners' sugar, then bake for 2 to 3 minutes until the sugar caramelizes. Leave to cool and coat in chocolate as for the *orangettes* below.

Tip. If you can't find any slivered almonds in the shops, make your own, cutting whole almonds lengthwise to make sticks.

Tuiles

Makes about 20
Preparation time: 30 minutes
Refrigeration time: 30 minutes to 1 hour
7 oz best quality chocolate (dark, white, or milk)
1 tbsp chopped toasted filberts, almonds, or slivered cocoa beans
A sheet of acetate (p. 144) or a sheet of waxed paper
A *tuiles* shaper (p. 144)

Melt the chocolate in a microwave oven or a bowl over hot water, then stir in the almonds, filberts, or slivered cocoa beans. On the sheet of acetate, shape the mixture into very thin disks in sets of 4. When the chocolate begins to set, use scissors to cut the acetate into strips for each set of 4 *tuiles* and place them on the *tuiles* shaper. Leave to set completely, then turn the *tuiles* over, and very carefully remove the plastic strip.

Orangettes

Makes about 30
Preparation time: 30 minutes
4 oz best quality dark chocolate
4 oz strips of candied orange peel
A sheet of acetate (p. 144) or a sheet of waxed paper

Melt the chocolate in a microwave oven or bowl over hot water. Dip one strip of candied orange peel in the chocolate at a time, coat it in chocolate, and allow any excess chocolate to drip back into the bowl. Leave to cool.

Orangettes

Molds

Small chocolate shapes

11 oz best quality chocolate
A sheet of acetate (p. 144)
An angled spatula (p. 144)

Temper the chocolate or melt it in a microwave oven or bowl over hot water. Pour into the mold, ensuring that each shape is filled and that all the chocolate is spread out by tapping the base of the mold for a few seconds to release any air bubbles that could spoil the surface of the chocolate shapes.

Scrape any excess chocolate off the mold onto the sheet of acetate, or alternatively into a large bowl. Take care not to leave any chocolate between the shapes, as this will make them more difficult to turn out and will make the shapes less well defined.

Leave the mold to cool at room temperature for a few minutes, then transfer to a cool place or a refrigerator for 30 minutes to 1 hour. They will be ready to turn out when the chocolate has come away from the edges.

To turn the chocolates out, twist the mold slightly as you would with an ice-cube tray. When the chocolate lifts, making a smart snap, you can carefully turn it over and remove the shapes. If you don't hear anything, refrigerate for a further 20 minutes.

Tip. If you have tempered the chocolate, the shapes will stay glossy; if not, they may tarnish after 24 hours, but even so they will without doubt still be edible! Use the remaining chocolate to make candies for example or, alternatively, to make cakes, mousses, or drinks.

Large chocolate shapes

7 oz best quality chocolate
A sheet of acetate (p. 144)

Temper or melt the chocolate (p. 143). Pour into the mold, tilting it to ensure that the inside is thoroughly coated. Place the mold on a sheet of acetate, allowing any excess chocolate to drip onto the acetate, then refrigerate for a few minutes.

Turn the mold over and leave to cool completely. Turn out of the mold as above.

To assemble the shape, soften the edges for a few seconds—on a warmed plate for example—and then stick the two pieces together.

Tip. It is best to use chocolate at a temperature of about 86° F, as otherwise the shape will be too delicate and will crack when being turned out.

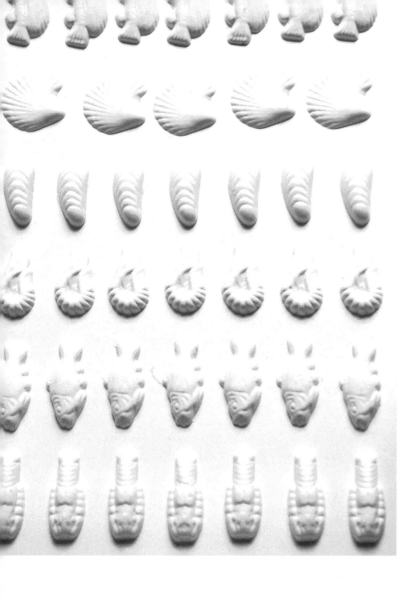

basics
for a carefree kitchen

Utensils and small equipment HERE IS A VERY SMALL SELECTION
OF PROFESSIONAL TOOLS THAT YOU WILL EASILY FIND IN SPECIALIST STORES.

1 Fluted or heart-shaped pastry cutters: use to make your petits-fours and shortbreads, or to create marzipan or fondant shapes.

2 Notched tomato scoop or apple corer: makes it easier to scoop the seeds out of cherry tomatoes and other small vegetables and fruits.

3 Apple slicer: it's so much quicker!

4 Stainless steel rings: use to assemble dishes, desserts, salads, and so on. A simple principle to achieve a great effect!

5 Zesters for left- or right-handed use: good for stripping ribbons of zest from citrus fruits and making attractive decorations with all sorts of vegetables.

6 Vegetable slice: cuts radishes into fan shapes.

7 Radish garnish maker: this is how professional chefs make those charming radish flowers.

8 Egg poacher: never again will the egg white ooze out into the simmering water!

9 Heart-shaped scoop: creates decorations and garnishes from apples, foie gras, and so on.

10 Aluminum baking beans: for baking tart shells blind. Better than lentils, dried beans, and other split peas because they distribute the heat perfectly, so the pastry bakes more evenly.

11 Shaped roller (or fluted pastry wheel, 11a): use it to create a pretty pattern or for cutting pastry or fresh pasta.

12 Butter curler: makes pretty curls and rolls.

13 Angled paring knife: for cutting out zigzag patterns.

Utensils: large equipment

1 I'm a great nonstick fan. But take care, it is fragile! Nowadays, there are all sorts of wonderful silicon coatings on which you can cook anything, right down to making your own caramel!

2 Wire racks are essential: for glazing, cooling, carrying.

3 Roasting rack: to prevent the meat sitting in its own fat. It is also very good for roasting little potatoes placed underneath.

4 A good cast-iron casserole: so that you can leave food gently simmering to perfection.

Hot sauces

Peanut and soy sauce

Serves 4 to 6
Preparation time: 5 minutes
Cooking time: 3 minutes
2 garlic cloves, finely chopped
1 tbsp soy sauce
4 tbsp crunchy peanut butter
1 tsp chili sauce
1 tsp ground cumin
1 tsp ground coriander
1 tsp ground ginger
1 tbsp lime juice
1 tsp sugar
1¼ cups water

Put all the ingredients in a pan, stir, and heat. Serve with noodles, vegetables, or broiled fish.

Bread sauce

Serves 6 to 8
Preparation time: 10 minutes
Cooking time: 15 minutes
1 onion
5 to 6 cloves
1⅝ cups milk
1 bay leaf
¼ stick butter
2½ cups fresh breadcrumbs
Salt and pepper

Stud the peeled onion with the cloves. Place in a pan with the milk, bay leaf, salt, and pepper, then bring to boiling point. Remove from the heat then add the breadcrumbs and the butter. Simmer gently for 10 minutes, stirring from time to time. Discard the onion and serve the sauce hot with poultry or game birds.

Tip. Make your own fresh breadcrumbs by whizzing stale bread in a blender.

Tomato sauce

Serves 6
Preparation time: 15 minutes
Cooking time: 25 minutes
1 garlic clove, finely chopped
1 lb large ripe tomatoes, skinned and seeded
or 1 lb 9 oz to 1 lb 12 oz canned tomatoes
1 tbsp olive oil
1 tbsp chopped parsley
1 tbsp chopped basil
1 tsp sugar
1 tsp tomato paste
2 tbsp red wine
Salt and black pepper

In a pan, brown the garlic in hot oil for a few moments, then add the finely chopped tomatoes, herbs, and sugar. Simmer for 10 minutes. Add the tomato paste and the wine. Cook for a further 15 minutes. Season to taste and serve with pasta or meat with a sprinkling of grated Parmesan or *pecorino* cheese.

Tip. Make your own tomato paste by blending sun-dried tomatoes to a paste in a blender or food processor.

Carbonara sauce

Serves 4
Preparation time: 15 minutes
1 tbsp butter
1 tbsp olive oil
1 cup diced bacon
4 very fresh egg yolks
3 tbsp light cream
¾ cup freshly grated Parmesan or *pecorino* cheese
Salt and pepper

Heat the butter and oil in a skillet and fry the diced bacon until golden. Drain on paper towels and keep warm. Beat the egg yolks together with the cream and half the cheese in a large bowl, then add the bacon. Pour the sauce over the hot pasta. Stir well, season with salt and pepper, and sprinkle with the remaining cheese before serving.

Tip. Your sauce will be better if you cut your bacon from a piece (instead of pre-sliced), preferably *prosciutto* from your butcher or an Italian delicatessen. You can also reserve an egg yolk to serve on top of the pasta.

Peanut and soy sauce

Bread sauce

F   Tomato sauce

Carbonara sauce

Cold sauces
HERE ARE A FEW IDEAS FOR VERY SPICY SAUCES TO USE AS MARINADES AND/OR TO SERVE WITH BARBECUED MEAT OR FISH.

Salsa verde

Serves 4 to 6
Preparation time: 10 minutes
1 green chile or green bell pepper
2 tbsp lemon juice
1 onion
1 garlic clove
1 tbsp chopped cilantro
1 tbsp chopped basil
1 tbsp chopped parsley
2 tbsp olive oil
Salt and pepper

Remove the seeds from the chile or bell pepper and chop very finely with the herbs, spices, and onion. Stir in the lemon juice. Then, using a whisk, gradually add the olive oil. Season with salt and pepper, then serve.

Cuban mojo

Serves 6
Preparation time: 10 minutes
10 garlic cloves
2 tbsp lime juice
2 tsp cumin
3 tbsp olive oil
Salt and pepper

Finely chop the garlic in a food processor. Add the lime juice and cumin, and blend. Transfer the mixture to a bowl, slowly pour the olive oil over the garlic mixture, then whisk as for a mayonnaise. Season and serve.

Sweet-and-sour salsa

Serves 4 to 6
Preparation time: 15 minutes
A dozen fragrant cherry tomatoes
1 mango
½ pineapple
2 tbsp chopped cilantro
1 red chile, seeded and finely diced
Grated zest and juice of 1 lemon
Salt and pepper

Finely dice the tomatoes, mango, and pineapple. Add the coriander, chile, and lemon zest and juice. Season and keep in a refrigerator until ready to serve.

Olive, orange, and onion salsa

Serves 4 to 6
Preparation time: 15 minutes
1 cup black olives, pitted
1 cup green olives, pitted
2 oranges
1 red onion
1 tbsp Italian (flat-leaf) parsley
Salt and pepper

Slice the olives lengthwise. Peel and quarter the oranges and dice the onion and finely chop the parsley. Season with salt and pepper. Gently mix all the ingredients together and leave for 30 minutes to 1 hour before serving to allow the flavors to develop.

Salsa *verde*

Cuban *mojo*

Sweet-and-sour salsa

Olive, orange, and onion salsa

167

Chutneys

Tomato chutney

Makes 8 to 10 jars
Preparation time: 30 minutes
Cooking time: 1 hour
2 lb 4 oz tomatoes
1 lb apples, finely chopped
1 cup raisins
1¼ cups sugar
1 tsp salt
½ tsp Cayenne pepper
2 whole cloves
7 oz onion, finely chopped
1 cup red wine vinegar

Blanch the tomatoes in boiling water for 2 minutes, then remove the skins. Put all the ingredients except the raisins in a large pan and cook over low heat for 30 minutes.
Add the raisins and cook for a further 30 minutes.

Greengage chutney

Makes 8 to 10 jars
Preparation time: 30 minutes
Cooking time: 2 hours
4 lb 8 oz greengages, or plums, pitted
14 oz cooking apples, cut into pieces
14 oz tomatoes, chopped
1¾ cups sugar
2 lb 4 oz onions, chopped
1¾ cups golden raisins
1¾ cups currants
1 tsp allspice
2 cups wine vinegar
1 whole clove

Gently heat the sugar and vinegar with the spices. Add all the remaining ingredients and simmer for about 2 hours.

Prune chutney

Makes 4 to 6 jars
Preparation time: 30 minutes
Cooking time: 1 hour
2 lb 4 oz prunes, pitted
1 onion, diced
2½ cups wine vinegar
1 tbsp salt
1 tsp ground ginger
2 oz mustard seeds
1 tsp Cayenne pepper
2 tsp allspice
2 cups sugar

Put the prunes, onion, salt, and spices in a large pan and add two thirds of the vinegar. Bring to boiling point and simmer over low heat for 30 minutes. Add the remaining vinegar and the sugar and reduce until the mixture becomes a thick purée.

Apple chutney

Makes 8 to 10 jars
Preparation time: 25 minutes
Cooking time: 25 minutes
5 lb 8 oz apples, cut into pieces
4 cups wine vinegar
11 oz onions, chopped
3½ cups golden raisins
2¾ cups brown sugar
3 tbsp salt
2 tsp ground ginger

Put all the ingredients in a large pan, bring to boiling point, and simmer for 25 minutes.

Crushed vegetables and potatoes
(*mash* where I come from)

WHAT? A WHOLE PAGE ON MASHED POTATOES? EVERYONE LOVES POTATOES, AND ALTHOUGH THEY DON'T HAVE A VERY COOL IMAGE, JUST DEFTLY ADD A FEW INGREDIENTS THAT COMPLEMENT THE REST OF THE DISH AND THEY ARE SURE TO GO DOWN WELL WITH YOUR GUESTS. THERE IS NO NEED TO GET OUT THE FOOD PROCESSOR, JUST CRUSH THEM WITH A POTATO MASHER OR EVEN A FORK FOR SMALL QUANTITIES. MASH REHEATS VERY WELL IN A MICROWAVE OVEN AND RETAINS ITS HEAT WELL IN A PAN WITH A LID ON. DON'T MAKE IT MORE THAN AN HOUR BEFORE THE MEAL.

Broccoli and filbert mashed potato

Serves 2 to 3
Preparation time: 10 minutes
Cooking time: 20 minutes
14 oz starchy potatoes, boiled
7 oz broccoli
1 tbsp chopped filberts
½ stick butter
Salt and pepper

Steam or boil the broccoli in salted water for about 10 minutes. Mash together with the potatoes, butter, salt, and pepper, then stir in the filberts.

Carrot and parsnip mash

Serves 2 to 3
Preparation time: 10 minutes
Cooking time: 20 minutes
11 oz carrots
11 oz parsnips
½ stick butter
Salt and pepper

Steam or boil the carrots and parsnips together in salted water. Drain, add the butter, and mash. Season and serve.

Coconut milk and cilantro mashed potato

Serves 2 to 3
Preparation time: 10 minutes
Cooking time: 20 minutes
14 oz starchy potatoes, boiled
5 tbsp coconut milk
3 tbsp chopped cilantro

Mash the potatoes with the coconut milk. Gently stir in the coriander and serve.

Onion and tomato mashed potato

Serves 2 or 3
Preparation time: 10 minutes
Cooking time: 20 minutes
14 oz starchy potatoes, boiled
7 oz small, ripe tomatoes
4 oz onions
3 tbsp olive oil
A knob of butter
Salt and pepper

Brown the onions in the oil and butter, then mash with the potatoes. Season. Halve or quarter the tomatoes, depending on size, and stir into the mashed potato mixture.

Carrot and parsnip mash

Coconut milk and cilantro
mashed potato

Flavored butters

THESE FLAVORED BUTTERS WILL KEEP FOR SEVERAL WEEKS IN A REFRIGERATOR. THEY ENHANCE THE FLAVOR OF BROILED MEAT OR FISH, AND ARE DELICIOUS SPREAD ON BREAD AND SERVED WITH SOUPS. YOU CAN CHOOSE ALL SORTS OF SHAPES. THEY TAKE ONLY 5 MINUTES TO MAKE, THEN CHILL THEM IN A REFRIGERATOR FOR ABOUT 1 HOUR. FOR ALL THESE RECIPES, YOU WILL NEED 2¾ STICKS BUTTER. BLEND ALL THE INGREDIENTS TOGETHER IN A FOOD PROCESSOR FOR 2 TO 3 MINUTES. WRAP THE MIXTURE IN PLASTIC WRAP AND SHAPE INTO A CYLINDER.

Cilantro and lime

2 or 3 tbsp finely chopped cilantro
Zest of 2 limes
Pepper

Sun-dried tomato, basil, and garlic

4 or 5 pieces of sun-dried tomato
3 or 4 tbsp basil
1 small garlic clove

Gorgonzola and black pepper

4 oz Gorgonzola
2 tbsp crushed black peppercorns

Walnut butter

2 tbsp finely chopped walnuts

Black pepper butter

2 tbsp crushed black peppercorns

Olive, rosemary, and thyme

⅔ cup pitted black olives
1 tsp finely chopped thyme
1 tsp finely chopped rosemary
Pepper

Cumin butter

2 tbsp toasted cumin seeds

Sweet spiced butter

3 tsp five-spice powder
2 tsp sugar

Savory spiced butter

½ tsp turmeric
½ tsp ground cumin
½ tsp ground ginger
½ tsp ground nutmeg
Freshly ground pepper

Pestos

JUST LIKE FRESH PASTA OR PIZZA DOUGH, PESTO SAUCE IS INCREDIBLY EASY TO MAKE AND SO MUCH BETTER THAN ANYTHING YOU CAN BUY IN THE SHOPS. THERE'S NOTHING TO IT. THE EFFORT/EFFECT RATIO IS EXCELLENT! IT IS DELICIOUS WITH PASTA, BUT ALSO WITH BROILED MEAT OR FISH. YOU CAN STIR IT INTO ONE OF THE MASH DISHES ON PAGE 170, OR USE IT TO FILL TARTLETS OR SAVORY PETITS-FOURS. MOST OF THESE RECIPES TAKE FIVE MINUTES TO MAKE AND SERVE FOUR PEOPLE. THERE ARE ENDLESS VARIATIONS. IT'S UP TO YOU TO DISCOVER DIFFERENT COMBINATIONS USING YOUR OWN FAVORITE HERBS AND DRIED FRUITS.

Walnut, pecorino, and Italian (flat-leaf) parsley

This version uses *pecorino* cheese instead of Parmesan.

Red pesto

Almonds, *manchego* cheese, sun-dried tomato, and basil

This is a Spanish version; *manchego* is a Spanish cheese similar to Parmesan. Use the same quantities and add a tablespoon of sun-dried tomatoes.

Traditional pine nut, basil, and Parmesan pesto

4 tbsp pine nuts
4 tbsp fresh Parmesan, cut into pieces
4 tbsp fresh basil
3 to 4 tbsp olive oil
Sea salt and black pepper

Blend all the ingredients together in a food processor to form a paste. Add more olive oil if the mixture is too thick.

Arugula pesto

2 oz arugula leaves
1 garlic clove
1 tbsp parsley
¼ cup pine nuts
1 tbsp Parmesan or *pecorino* cheese
4 to 5 tbsp olive oil

Tip. Play around with the textures. Basil is always better reduced to a purée with the olive oil; avoid overprocessing it, as it easily turns black. You can finely mince the cheese and pine nuts instead of blending them.

Walnut, *pecorino*, and Italian parsley

Red pesto

Arugula pesto

Traditional pine nut, basil, and Parmesan pesto

Vegetables with a difference

Roasted vegetables

Serves 6
Preparation time: 10 minutes
Cooking time: 1 hour
2 tomatoes
1 eggplant
1 or 2 bell peppers
1 or 2 zucchini
1 red or white onion
1 or 2 garlic cloves
1 tsp thyme
1 sprig of rosemary
4 to 5 tbsp olive oil
Salt and pepper

Preheat the oven to 400° F.
Cut the vegetables into large chunks and drizzle with the olive oil. Season. Roast for about 1 hour, turning them over several times until they are golden and even blackened in places.

Tip. Different colored peppers make an attractive dish. As for the garlic, make the most of it; it is delicious roasted, and very good for the digestion

Caramelized tomatoes

Serves 4 to 6
Preparation time: 5 minutes
Cooking time: 1½ hours
A dozen small, ripe Italian tomatoes
3 tbsp olive oil
1 tbsp superfine sugar

Preheat the oven to 300° F. Halve the tomatoes and place side by side in a shallow ovenproof dish. Combine the olive oil and sugar, and drizzle over the tomatoes. Bake for about 1½ hours. The caramel that forms on the bottom of the dish is a sheer delight!

Roasted vegetables   Caramelized tomatoes

177

Ring the changes with salad dressings AN

ORIGINAL DRESSING CAN TRANSFORM EVEN THE BLANDEST OF SALADS. IF YOU'RE ANYTHING LIKE ME—IN OTHER WORDS, NINE TIMES OUT OF TEN YOU FORGET TO MAKE IT BEFORE THE MEAL—ALWAYS HAVE A GOOD OLIVE OIL AND A GOOD BALSAMIC VINEGAR IN THE HOUSE.

Thyme, rosemary, and wine vinegar dressing

Serves 6
Preparation time: 5 minutes
1¼ cups olive oil
1 tbsp red wine vinegar
1 tbsp Dijon mustard
1 tsp sugar
1 tsp thyme
1 tsp rosemary
Sea salt and black pepper

Blend the thyme and rosemary seeds in a food processor or crush them with a mortar and pestle. Put all the ingredients in a bowl and combine with a whisk.

Lebanese dressing

Serves 6
Preparation time: 5 minutes
3 tbsp olive oil
2 tbsp *tahini* (sesame seed paste)
Juice of 2 lemons
1 garlic clove, finely chopped
1 tbsp chopped Italian (flat-leaf) parsley
1 tbsp chopped mint
Sea salt and black pepper

Combine the oil with the *tahini* and lemon juice. Add the remaining ingredients.

Balsamic vinegar dressing

Serves 4
Preparation time: 2 minutes
4 tbsp olive oil
1 tbsp balsamic vinegar
Sea salt and black pepper

Pour the vinegar into a bowl, add the oil, mix well, and season.

Lemon and parsley dressing

Serves 6
Preparation time: 5 minutes
Juice of 2 lemons
5 tbsp olive oil
3 tbsp finely chopped Italian (flat-leaf) parsley
Sea salt and black pepper

Whisk the oil and lemon juice together. Add the parsley and season.

Tapenade dressing

Serves 6
Preparation time: 5 minutes
7 to 8 tbsp olive oil
3 tbsp red wine vinegar
4 tbsp black olive *tapenade*
Pepper

Thoroughly combine the *tapenade* and vinegar in a bowl. Slowly add the olive oil, beating constantly. Season with pepper.

Thai dressing

Serves 6
Preparation time: 10 minutes
Juice of 2 limes
5 tbsp grapeseed oil
2 tsp *nuoc-mâm*
2 tbsp chopped cilantro
½ red chile, seeded and finely chopped
1 sprig of lemon grass
3 chive blades
Salt and pepper

Combine the oil, lime juice, and *nuoc-mâm*, then incorporate the remaining ingredients.

Chicken, vegetable, or fish stock MOST OF THE STOCKS
THAT YOU WILL NEED FOR YOUR SAUCES, SOUPS, GRAVIES, AND SO ON SHOULD BE MADE IN ADVANCE. THAT WAY, YOU CAN MAKE YOUR DISHES WITHOUT RESORTING TO THE PRODUCTS SOLD IN SUPERMARKETS. HOMEMADE STOCK WILL KEEP FOR 3 OR 4 DAYS IN A REFRIGERATOR, A FEW MONTHS EVEN IN A FREEZER, OR YOU CAN STORE IT IN SMALL QUANTITIES TO USE AS YOU NEED IT.

Chicken stock

Makes about 6 cups
Preparation time: 10 minutes
Cooking time: 2 hours
1 chicken, weighing about 3½ lbs
1 onion studded with cloves
2 leeks, sliced
2 carrots, sliced
2 stalks of celery, with leaves, chopped
1 bay leaf
12 cups water
5 black peppercorns

Put all the ingredients into a stockpot. Slowly bring to boiling point, then immediately reduce the heat. Cover and leave to simmer for about 1½ hours, removing any scum that forms with a slotted spoon. Leave to cool for about 30 minutes. Using paper towels, remove any fat that may have formed on the surface, then strain the stock. Discard any solids remaining in the pan.

Fish stock

Makes about 4 cups
Preparation time: 10 minutes
Cooking time: 25 minutes
2 lb 4 oz fish bones
3 shallots, finely chopped
¼ stick butter
9 oz small mushrooms, chopped
2 carrots, sliced
1 leek, sliced
6 cups water
A bouquet garni

Put all the ingredients in a large pan and slowly bring to boiling point. Simmer for 25 minutes, removing any scum that forms with a slotted spoon. Leave to cool, then strain.

Tip. Fish bones give a bitter taste if left to cook for too long.

Vegetable stock

Makes about 6 cups
Preparation time: 10 minutes
Cooking time: 30 minutes
1 lb onions, thinly sliced
1 lb carrots, sliced
4 stalks of celery, with leaves, coarsely chopped
8 cups water
A bouquet garni
10 white peppercorns
¼ stick butter

Melt the butter in a large stockpot.
Fry the vegetables lightly, but do not allow them to turn golden or to burn, as that would ruin the flavor of the stock.
Add the water, pepper, and bouquet garni, and slowly bring to boiling point.
Reduce the heat, remove any scum that may be produced using a slotted spoon, then half cover and leave to simmer very gently for 1 or 2 hours.
Pass the stock through a fine strainer and leave to cool.

Chicken stock

Pastry

Plain pastry

To make a pastry shell about 11 inches in diameter
Preparation time: 10 minutes
Refrigeration time: 2 hours
2 cups all-purpose flour
1¼ sticks cold butter
2 tbsp superfine sugar (omit for savory tarts)
3 tbsp very cold water

Place the flour and butter in a food processor and combine until the mixture resembles breadcrumbs. Add the water and continue mixing for a few seconds.
Shape into a ball and wrap in plastic wrap.
Leave to rest in a refrigerator for 2 hours.

Sweet pastry

To make a pastry shell about 11 inches in diameter
Preparation time: 10 minutes
Refrigeration time: 3 hours
2 cups all-purpose flour
1¼ sticks cold butter, cut into pieces
4 egg yolks
½ cup superfine sugar
A pinch of baking powder

Whisk the eggs and sugar until the mixture is pale and frothy. Add the butter, followed by the sifted flour and baking powder. Using the finger tips, blend the ingredients together.
Shape into a ball, cover with plastic wrap, and place in a refrigerator for 2 to 3 hours.

Chocolate pastry

To make a pastry shell about 11 inches in diameter
Preparation time: 10 minutes
Refrigeration time: 2 hours
2 cups all-purpose flour
1¾ sticks unsalted butter
1 cup confectioners' sugar
7 tbsp cocoa powder
1 egg yolk
1 tbsp cold water

Pour the flour into a bowl, make a well in the center, and add all the remaining ingredients. Combine well using a fork. Knead to form a smooth dough. Shape into a ball, wrap in plastic wrap, and leave to rest in a refrigerator for 2 hours.

Ultra rich pastry (gourmets' special)

To make a pastry shell about 11 inches in diameter
Preparation time: 10 minutes
Refrigeration time: 3 hours
2 cups all-purpose flour
3 egg yolks
¾ cup confectioners' sugar
2 tbsp light cream
1½ sticks unsalted butter, cut into pieces and softened

Beat together the cream, eggs, and sugar. Add the butter and mix well. Gradually add the flour, working the mixture with the fingertips until the mixture resembles slightly compacted fine breadcrumbs. Quickly shape into a ball on a floured surface. Wrap in plastic wrap and place in a refrigerator for 3 hours.

Pasta

ADMITTEDLY, IT TAKES A LITTLE TIME AND EFFORT TO MAKE YOUR OWN PASTA, BUT THE TASTE IS BEYOND COMPARE AND, ONCE YOU'VE GOT THE KNACK, THERE'LL BE NO STOPPING YOU. GET YOURSELF A LITTLE HAND-OPERATED PASTA MACHINE—MOST PLACES SELL THEM NOW. IF THAT'S REALLY ASKING TOO MUCH OF YOU, DO TRY TO BUY FRESH PASTA FROM ITALIAN DELICATESSENS OR THE LARGER SUPERMARKETS.

Pasta dough

Serves 4 as a main dish, 6 as an appetizer or side dish
Preparation time: 5 minutes
Resting time: 30 to 60 minutes
4⅓ cups all-purpose flour
4 eggs
1 tsp olive oil
4 or 5 tbsp water

Place all the ingredients in a food processor and combine until the mixture forms a large ball.

Knead for a further 1 or 2 minutes until the dough is very elastic. Cover with plastic wrap and leave to rest for between 30 and 60 minutes. Roll out the dough and cut into rectangles the same width as your pasta machine.

Pass the rectangles through the machine 3 or 4 times, folding them up again each time to produce a very smooth dough. Adjust the setting to make lasagna, fettucine, or spaghetti, and so on.

1

2

3

glossary
index

glossary

arugula

A real star in the past few years, this salad leaf is highly prized for its strong, peppery taste. It goes wonderfully with sweet/savory mixtures, such as fruit/meat, or smoked chicken. With its long leaves, it is good for creating stunning presentations. It is now available all year round in plastic bags from your supermarket.

baby spinach leaves

Crisp, but with a mild flavor, they are delicious in salads, either on their own or combined with other leaves. They are now readily available in supermarkets but, if you can't find any, you can use watercress or lambs' lettuce instead.

bagels

Golden dry rolls shaped rather like a doughnut. Bagels are cooked twice, first in boiling water, after which they are brushed with beaten egg and then baked in the oven.

baking powder

This is a mixture of baking soda and acid (usually cream of tartar). The raising agent releases carbon dioxide when it comes into contact with water and is used in recipes that contain little or no egg white to achieve a light, airy consistency. Available from grocers and supermarkets.

balsamic vinegar

This glossy vinegar is made from cooked grape must. It is almost black, with a sweet and woody flavor, and is aged in wooden casks to give it its distinctive aroma. Highly prized today, it is sold in groceries and supermarkets. Try to track down *aceto balsamico di Modena*, easily the best and most refined.

black bread

You will find this very compact German bread made from black rye sold in packets in the supermarket bread section.

bulgur

This is one of the essential ingredients of Middle-Eastern cuisine. It is made from sprouted wheat, which is then boiled, dried, and crushed—hence its other name of cracked wheat. It swells and softens when soaked and is the basic ingredient of *tabbouleh*. You will find it in your supermarket.

cranberry juice

Highly valued in Britain as well as the United States and Canada. It is a clear juice, not overly sweet, very thirst quenching, and full of vitamins. It is a bit like pomegranate juice in color and flavor. Children love it. You can find it in supermarkets and delicatessens.

cream

There are three main types of cream, which vary in use depending on their fat content. Heavy cream has a high fat content of 36–40 percent and can be whipped to a firm consistency to fill or decorate cakes, for example. Light whipping cream has a fat content of 30–36 percent and is less rich than heavy cream. When whipped, it is good for making ice creams, soufflés, and mousses, where a light, airy consistency is required. Light cream has the lowest fat content, 18–30 percent, and therefore cannot be whipped. It is excellent for soups and sauces.

crème fraîche

Many of the recipes in this book that list sour cream in the ingredients could use crème fraîche instead but this product is not readily available in the United States. However, if you would like to experiment, the following recipe is a very good substitute: Combine 1 cup whipping cream and 2 tbsp buttermilk in a glass container. Cover and let stand at room temperature (about 70° F) for 8–24 hours or until very thick. Stir well and store in the refrigerator for 10 days maximum.

feta

This fresh, grainy, Greek sheep's milk cheese is preserved in a mixture of whey and brine. Delicious in salads, savory pies, or puff pastry parcels.

fresh ginger

This rhizome with its twisted shapes and spicy flavor is essential for Southeastern Asian and Middle-Eastern cookery. You need to remove the woody skin. Available from delicatessens, Asian food stores, or alongside the chiles and exotic fruits in your supermarket. It will keep for several weeks in a refrigerator. Preserved ginger, which is very sweet, but spicy and strong, is used in confectionery and pastry-making. Available from Asian food stores and supermarkets.

ganache

This is a mixture of cream and chocolate. Ganache is more or less malleable depending on the proportion of cream used. To make a cake filling, more cream is required than would be the case with truffles. As soon as the mixture has cooled, it can be whipped to obtain a more mousse-like consistency. You usually make your own ganache, but it can be bought ready-made from suppliers to the chocolate-making trade.

hummus

Hummus means "chickpeas" in Arabic and takes several forms. The most commonly found recipe involves combining chickpeas (garbanzo beans), olive oil, garlic, lemon juice, and sesame seed purée (tahini). You can, however, make your own mixture using different ingredients to make a dip or any other starter. Chickpeas are readily available, but it may be more difficult to track down the tahini. Try supermarkets, delicatessens, and Asian or Middle-Eastern food stores.

maple syrup

This great classic with its sweet/sour taste goes wonderfully with pancakes and waffles, but also with savory dishes. Avoid the many imitations (called *jus de poteaux* or "wooden post juice" in Canada), and try to find the real thing; there really is no comparison! Available from supermarkets and delicatessens.

mascarpone

This extremely rich and creamy Italian cheese is a bit like crème fraîche, but even smoother and less bitter. It can be replaced by crème fraîche in all dishes except tiramisu. Available from the supermarket cheese section and delicatessens.

peanut butter

A great American classic, this spread only merits its reputation for being junk food if you eat it with jelly in a sandwich, which many people do. With the distinctive flavor and smooth consistency provided by the peanuts, it enriches Thai dishes. Crunchy peanut butter has the added benefit of its crisp texture.

pecans

This nut originates and is much used in the southern states of America. It looks a bit like a walnut, but is less bitter in flavor and more elongated in shape. You can nearly always use walnuts instead. Pecans can usually be found in traditional groceries and in the dried fruit section of supermarkets.

Pimms

Its bitter taste is slightly reminiscent of red vermouth. In England, it is traditionally drunk with lemon/lime soda or tonic water, together with slices of citrus fruit, fresh mint, and/or cucumber. Available from good liquor stores or via the internet.

pine nuts

These are the soft, white, sweet seeds produced in the cones of pine trees such as the European Swiss stone pine, *pinus cembra*. They form the basis of Italian pesto and can be added to salads. They are even better toasted. You will find them in the dried fruit section of your supermarket.

pita

Pockets of white unleavened bread that can be split open for the filling to be added and can contain even fairly liquid mixtures without becoming disastrously soft. Available from the bread section of supermarkets.

potatoes

You need starchy potatoes for making mash to absorb the butter and cream. However, the smooth-skinned varieties are best for making potato salad so that the dressing doesn't get completely absorbed, making the potatoes go soggy.

prosciutto

This Italian salted, cured, and air-dried ham has a mellow flavor. Usually very thinly sliced, it is now available from most supermarkets. If you cannot find it, use any other finely sliced, raw ham instead.

red onion

Less strong and often larger than the white or yellow onion, this variety can be cooked in the same way as the others. To make the most of its beautiful color, it is best to use the red onion raw, as it tends to turn black when cooked for any length of time. Available everywhere.

Scandinavian bread

A soft, white, and slightly sweet Swedish bread. If you cannot find it in your supermarket, use ordinary sliced bread instead.

sesame seeds

Seeds from the Middle East with a pleasant hazelnut (filbert) flavor. Excellent toasted then sprinkled over some bread or to give a crispy texture to vegetables, pasta, or salads. The seeds are reduced to a paste to make tahini, an ingredient used to make hummus. Available from delicatessens and supermarkets.

star anise

As its name suggests, this is an extremely beautiful, star-shaped spice produced from a Chinese citrus fruit. Its intense aroma is reminiscent of both aniseed and fennel. It is one of the ingredients of five-spice powder. It can be used in moderation with fish and shellfish. Available from delicatessens and supermarkets.

sun-dried tomatoes

Becoming increasingly popular, they have a powerful, fruity flavor, enriching stews, pasta sauces, and salads. You can find them dried, preserved in oil, or even in purée form. Available from delicatessens or from the supermarket.

tapenade

This savory olive, caper, and anchovy spread from the Provence region of France is delicious served on slices of toasted French bread with a glass of champagne! It can also be used as a filling for hard-cooked eggs.

index

Kitchen utensils and cooking ingredients, long the preserve of the professionals, now available to you to treat your family and friends and to make your life easier.

Three types of chocolate couverture, praline, cocoa bean slivers and essential chocolate making tools, to create delicious desserts, chocolates and original décor, all in your home.

We also offer dried fruits and spices as well as a complete line of professional cooking utensils.

For a copy of our catalogue

visit our website: www.aucomptoirdeschefs.com